Dr Jonathan Bell is Head Curator at the Ulster Folk and Transport Museum, where he has worked since 1976. He has published widely on the history of Irish rural society, and associated farming methods. Fieldwork has always been a key element of his work, and this has led to the collection of oral testimonies throughout Ulster and other parts of Ireland, many of which have been used in writing this book.

Members of the McSparran family at Knocknacarry, County Antrim, in 1935

Ulster Farming Families
1930–1960

Jonathan Bell

ULSTER HISTORICAL FOUNDATION
IN ASSOCIATION
WITH THE
ULSTER FOLK AND TRANSPORT MUSEUM

Ulster Historical Foundation is pleased to acknowledge support for this publication provided by the Ulster Folk and Transport Museum (MAGNI).

First Published 2005
by the Ulster Historical Foundation
12 College Square East, Belfast BT1 6DD
www.ancestryireland.com
www.booksireland.org.uk

Printed by Cromwell Press
Design by CheahDesign

This book is dedicated to
Dermot Francis
1960–2003
Ar dheis Dé go raibh a anam uasal

Joe Kane with a young horse, at Drumkeeran, County Fermanagh, in the 1930s
(L2727/3)

Contents

Jean and John Tyrrell with a Large White Ulster pig on their farm in
Cloughan, Cogry, in 1935

Introduction

This book is based on oral accounts of life on family farms in Ulster during the mid-twentieth century. Most interviews were recorded in the 1970s and 1980s, during fieldwork undertaken by my colleague Mervyn Watson and myself, as part of our work in the Ulster Folk and Transport Museum (Fig. 1). The period between 1930 and 1960 was chosen for the study because many older people could clearly remember these decades.

When we attempt to interpret any historical period, we can either emphasise its distinctive character or present it as part of an ongoing process, which can be understood only by looking at events that came before and after. Either emphasis could be justified in studying the mid-twentieth century. One of the great cataclysms of history, the Second World War, dominated the period, yet from a farming point of view the major influences of the war were its acceleration of technical innovation, and the programme of government intervention that it entrenched. In general, changes that took place during the period were part of a process of modernisation that gained momentum in the early eighteenth century, and has been ongoing ever since.

Fig. 1 Joe Kane of Drumkeeran, County Fermanagh being interviewed by Mervyn Watson of the Ulster Folk and Transport Museum in 1986 (L3133/2/7)

We could be even more far-reaching in situating the period between 1930 and 1960 in a wider historical context. Estyn Evans's seminal work on Irish folkways was largely based on fieldwork carried out in the 1930s and 1940s, when he was intrigued to observe farming techniques still in use that almost certainly had been practised since prehistoric times. (For example, archaeological research has confirmed that techniques such as the use of cultivation ridges and the construction of dry stone walls, still practised in parts of Ireland, go back as far as the third millennium BC.) Evans saw the rural world that he investigated as having a 'prehistoric substratum', which still had a profound influence on cultural practices, attitudes and beliefs.[1] Many of us find this an extravagant claim, which is largely impossible to prove or disprove, but Evans's imagination was obviously fired by the aura of great antiquity that he sensed in many artefacts and practices at the time. The Irish language was still spoken in parts of the Sperrin Mountains, as well as along the western seaboard of Donegal, as it had been for at least two thousand years. In the Glens of Antrim it was possible to see wheelless slide cars (Fig. 2) and solid wheel 'cars', vehicles with very ancient pedigrees, in daily use, and Cushendall hill ponies, the sturdy descendants of medieval Gaelic *gearráin*, were still fairly common in coastal Antrim.

The development of local historical studies has made us much more aware of regional variations within Ireland, and there are areas in Ulster that are still seen as having a distinctive character. At the beginning of the new millennium, however, it has become difficult to imagine the extent of these variations, as they were taken for granted sixty years ago. The Glens of Antrim, the Mourne mountains, the Fermanagh lakes and the west of County Donegal were just some of the areas seen – by both visitors and the people who lived there – as having their own unique character.

The sense of regional distinctiveness is well expressed in poetry from the period. In the 1930s, for example, Patrick Kavanagh described the world contained within his home farm in Monaghan:

> My black hills have never seen the sun rising,
> Eternally they look north towards Armagh …
> They are my Alps and I have climbed the Matterhorn
> With a sheaf of hay for three perishing calves.[2]

In 1950, Belfastman John Hewitt included the following in a poem about Glenaan in the Glens of Antrim:

> … I stop
> to name the peaks along their dark array,
> for these are more than mountains shouldered clear
> into the sharp star-pointed atmosphere,
> into the sunset. They mark out and bound
> the utmost limits of my chosen ground.[3]

Since the mid-twentieth century, the countryside has been transformed to such an extent that many traces of past life have been obliterated. The spread of cities, new towns, motorways, forestry schemes, and draining and clearing of land are large-scale examples of massive transformation. The development of visitor amenities might seem to be less destructive in its effects than that of industry and agri-business, but the provision of an infrastructure to support tourism can also lead to a radical disjunction between the present and even the recent past. A clear instance of this can be found around Sheephaven Bay in north Donegal. In the early twentieth century, members of the farming families of the Hornhead peninsula on the north-west of the bay built their own houses, used locally made carts and boats, made their own butter and bread, cured their own bacon, and trained their own horses. They supplemented their farming income in a wide variety of ways, including migrant labour, fishing, trapping rabbits and selling turf. One man, Hugh Strain, caught and trained falcons, which were then sent to England to be sold. His neighbour, Mick McHugh, recounted the following incident:

Fig. 2 Dan Laverty and his sister Kathleen bringing home turf on a slide car, near Waterfoot in the Glens of Antrim. The photograph was taken in 1952 by some naval cadets, who met the young people by chance on the mountain

> I knew him to be out fishing all night, and somebody told him there was a pair of falcon nesting at Melmore, and he put a currach into the water and rowed to Melmore, and he went up the cliffs and had four falcon hawks in the currach coming back. And he told me that as he was coming back across the bay, there lit one of them wee honey bees … on the stern of the currach and rested with his cargo of honey … and Hughie rowed on until he came to that house on Hornhead there, [and the bee flew off] … he was out of one of the skeps [beehives] there.[4]

This little incident evokes a way of life that would be unrecognisable in the same area in the new millennium. The coastal lowlands around Sheephaven are now visually congested with smart bijou residences, mostly second homes, used by their owners for only a few weeks each year. Currachs have been replaced by wind surfers and jet-skis, and the area is known as a place for wonderful family holidays. No one should regret the passing of the poverty that was so common in the past, and it is important to emphasise the happiness that modern visitors experience when staying in the area. However, the lack of a clear connection between the new world and the one that it has displaced is often shocking. It is almost as if the ways of life of sixty years ago might never have been.

The oral testimonies that form the core of this book capture the ambiguity of the period described: an era when the modern world of global production and bureaucracy coexisted with a small-scale, intimate world, in which links with the past were often strikingly apparent. The model of farming life from the testimonies included is a very positive one. This is not an attempt to present Ulster rural society in the recent past as a well-oiled functionalist machine. The book's main subject is the range of strategies adopted by farmers attempting to keep their farms viable. These related to planning the appropriate mix of crop and livestock production, the techniques to be used, and the division of labour required. All of this had both positive and negative effects on the local environment and way of life. Conflicts between people were common, and some of these were very deep. Individuals in the countryside are as likely to be brutal, vindictive and selfish as townspeople. In the case studies presented here, however, what emerges is an underlying decency that accurately reflects the character of the people who so generously allowed their memories to be included.

More than 130 tapes on farming were made during fieldwork, and the data in these have been used to suggest some generalisations. A smaller number of testimonies have been selected as case studies and examples. The people who allowed these to be recorded are listed in the appendix at the end of the book, along with references to the subjects that they discussed, and their location in the text. All the people who agreed to help deserve thanks.

Many friends and colleagues are owed thanks for help with the book, apart from those interviewed. Mr John Cooke, Mr Gilbert Patterson, Mrs Mary Savage, Mr Tommy Watt of Shetland Museums Service, Mr Terry MacDonald and Mr David Bigger provided photographs, and Museum Photographic Staff produced excellent work, as usual. Seamus O'Kane, Finbar McCormick, Fred Coll, Malachy McSparran, Eleanor Jordan, Philip

Flanagan, Olga McKeown and Allister McQuoid all helped museum staff to contact people for inclusion. Within the Museum, thanks are due to Marshall McKee for his enthusiastic support and to Maureen Paige, who went beyond the call of duty, as always. Mervyn Watson was so closely involved with the project, from fieldwork to publication, that it is hard to say where his work ended and my own began.

1. Country people talking

This book is about the past, and the way people talk about the past. It outlines some important changes in the lives of Ulster country people in the mid-twentieth century, and it does this mainly by using the oral testimonies of the people who experienced them.

One of the central aims of the book is to communicate the richness of the experiences recounted by farm people. Oral history is rightly celebrated for the wealth of evidence to which it allows access. In our society, even very literate people spend little time recording their own experiences, and until the very recent past, the experiences of people such as small farmers were rarely considered of sufficient importance to record. Oral history gives us access not only to the details of what happened to people, but also to their ambitions and emotions, either recalled from the time or reviewed in later life. It extends history to areas where written records often allow only informed speculation. However, some questions arise when we use this kind of source material, the most important of which relate to historical accuracy. Some of the key issues facing oral historians are outlined in Chapter 8; in the present chapter we will examine how the accounts used were presented and structured by the people interviewed.

Fig. 3 Dolly and Isabel Lyons, at Gannoway, County Down, in 1934 (L2726/8)

The amount and complexity of data collected during the fieldwork carried out in preparation for this book could allow many different types of analysis. One important aspect of the testimonies, which can be mentioned only briefly here, relates to the particular way in which the people included expressed themselves. In our society, urban middle-class people sometimes refer to themselves satirically as 'the chattering classes'. Anyone coming from this world, where words are strung together in a linear elaboration, can find the way many older country people talk unusual and even disconcerting. A long silence may precede, or arise during, a conversation, and people will describe some of the most important experiences in their lives with a brevity of expression that can seem understated to the point of bluntness.

Spare descriptions may, however, highlight deeply felt experience. A fine, and very happy, example of this was given by Isabel Lyons and her sister Dolly McRoberts, who grew up on a farm at Gannoway, County Down (Fig. 3). Isabel and her father, William Lyons, used to polish the horses' harness together. It was obviously one of her happiest memories. However, the delight that Isabel and Dolly took in recollecting this was expressed more in the detail of the memory than in directly emotional terms. Harness for the farm's working horses was kept in the stable, and that for the farm's pony in the scullery. It was here that Isabel and her father polished the harness every week, using *Brasso* and black boot-polish. William Lyons was known as a skilled horseman, and the brasses on the harness were always kept 'as if they were going out to a show'. The happiness in this family was also expressed in the sisters' description of their relationship to the farm's animals. There were four girls in the house, and no boys. Unusually, both Dolly and Isabel helped with training the farm's heavy horses (Fig. 4). Neither could remember any difficulty arising from this, because the horses 'were more or less kept as pets as well … They were sort of nursed … You'd be talking to them all the time.'

Country people often delight in stoical and inexpressive statements. Isabel and Dolly's parents had a love match. The women laughed with pleasure remembering conversations between their father and mother. They recounted how their father would say to their mother, 'I think I'll go up and see how the corn is doing. Are you coming with me?' She replied, 'Sure we were up last night.' 'Aw, come on up anyway.'

Fig. 4 William Lyons with daughters Dolly and Isabel at Gannoway, County Down, in 1933. Dolly is holding the horse's leg, and Isabel is holding the reins (L2726/5)

How people structured their accounts also pointed to possible differences between town and country. The ways in which family histories and the history of their immediate neighbourhoods were recounted can to some extent be related to the size and affluence of the particular family farm. Larger, wealthier farms tended to be better documented than smaller ones, for both business and inheritance purposes. The existence of documentation, sometimes stretching back several generations, was obviously used by people in relating a farm's history. However, the close connection that often exists between the history of a family and the history of their farm meant that in almost all cases family members were well informed about how their family came to live on a holding, and when. This awareness of general family history provided a context for personal accounts, which is often much more developed than the contexts available in many urban situations. The following examples give some of the ways in which people constructed the general history of their family farms.

Gerry McCormick's account of his family history

A connection between a family and a particular farm may in some cases be very recent. The late Gerry McCormick, who became manager of the Mona Creameries in Monaghan, explained the particular situation that led his family to establish themselves in the county:

> I was born actually in Donegal and my parents came to Rockcorry in the 1930s, so I'm not really a Monaghan man at all. My father … was brought up in Barnes Gap [County Donegal] … Three of my family were born in Belfast, two were born in Coatbridge in Scotland, and two were born in Ballybofey in Donegal … My father was RIC. He couldn't go back to Donegal in that troubled time because they took a very poor view of RIC men … Three of my family were born when he was serving in Belfast … So then he retired in 1921 after the Treaty, and he moved to Scotland …
>
> My mother was from Monaghan …[My father moved there. He] was interested in farming, being a Donegal man, and he wanted a bit of land for the cow – he had seven of a family you see, and he had to give them a drop of milk, and he was going buying milk here and there, and he said, 'Sure, you can buy a cow for ten pound!' And he bought the cow … so he took Cox's land up the road. Why it was called Cox's land, I don't know … three or four ones owned it … But, in 1937 or 1938, he bought the farm known as Ranaghan's … Every circus that came, they just seemed to … put their horses on it, no one seemed to care about it, so he bought the thirty acres for about eighty pound … And then that was our spread.

Malachy McSparran's account of his family history

The history of McSparran's farm is, in contrast to Gerry McCormick's account, a story of the slow development of one of the most prosperous farms in the Glens of Antrim. The current farmer, Malachy McSparran (Fig. 5), has recorded its history in detail and can recount the documentary and oral history of his family farm, back to the 1790s. This can be related to the length of time that his family has lived on the farm, and the amount of documentation that they have preserved, as well as their high level of education. Malachy

Fig. 5 Stack building on the McSparran farm at Drumnacur, County Antrim, in 1963. Malachy McSparran is on the right, Jim O'Neill, a farm labourer, is in the centre, and Charlie McAuley, another labourer, is on the left (L3090/4)

is also a well-known local historian: given all these factors, it is not surprising that he has investigated his family's history in a systematic way.[1]

North-east Antrim has ancient and complex historical links with western Scotland; the history of the McSparran family shows that these links have continued into modern times. Malachy McSparran's great-great-grandfather, Archibald, came from Gigha, a Scottish island that lies off the west coast of the Mull of Kintyre. Archie McSparran came to Antrim in 1792 and married a local woman, Anne McNeill, who had a farm in the Layde area, in the townland of Cornafurphy. His son John inherited this farm. Another son, James, Malachy McSparran's great-grandfather, went to sea as a merchant, trading from his own boat. His trade was based in Ardrossan in Scotland, and most of his work involved shipping merchandise between Ireland and Scotland. Like his father, he married an Antrim woman, Margaret McCormack. She had two brothers, each of whom had a farm of around twenty acres. Both men died unmarried, and Margaret's son James, Malachy McSparran's grandfather, inherited their farms.

Like his father, James McSparran developed business interests that were based in Scotland. He opened a shop in Commerce Street, Glasgow (Fig. 6), which supplied ships with salted fish, sugar, and other food necessary for voyages, which might last up to three months. The shop also carried on a local trade in groceries.

While James McSparran was working, he lived partly in Glasgow and partly in Ireland, where he was member of Antrim County Council. Between 1886 and 1901, he bought three farms in the Cushendun area; these, along with the farms he had inherited, were worked by two labourers. Further purchases were also made. A farm in Layde was bought and then sold to a brother-in-law, a sea captain who wished to invest in land. In 1917, a farm of twenty acres was bought in the townland of Knocknacarry. (In 1947, the McSparran family bought another farm, of twenty-four acres, in Knocknacarry.) In 1918, James McSparran retired to the farm at Cloney. His sons were not interested in continuing the business in Glasgow, and this was sold. Two of the sons were each given a house belonging to the farms at Knocknacarry. When James McSparran died in 1924 at the age of sixty-eight, farms in Inispollan and Clady townlands were inherited by one son, while Malachy McSparran's father, Archibald, who was trained in the agricultural college at Bellewstown, County Galway, inherited farms in the townlands of Cloney, Knocknacarry, Carnasheeran and Drumnacur. He also inherited a farm at Ballybrack from his mother, who in turn had inherited it from an unmarried brother. Archibald McSparran had five daughters and one son. When he died in 1983, aged eighty-seven, his son Malachy inherited the farms.

Fig. 6 McSparrans' shop, Commercial Street, Glasgow (L3090/7)

Joe Kane's account of his family history

Joe Kane's farm in Drumkeeran, County Fermanagh is one of the smallest in the accounts on which this book is based. Joe did not have the kind of documentary records that were available on the McSparran farm. However, like Malachy McSparran, Joe was a keen recorder of local history. He expressed this by emphasising the history of the townland of Drumkeeran, rather than his family history, which in his account goes no further back than a brief mention of his grandparents.

Joe Kane was born in 1913 in Drumkeeran, about one mile north-west of the town of Ederney. During his childhood there were eight families living in Drumkeeran, making up a population of about forty-five people. Farms in the area varied greatly in size. One large stock farm extended over more than 100 acres, while two other farms, which Joe Kane considered to have been commercially viable, were between thirty and forty acres in area. The smallest farms were between fourteen and seventeen acres, and were not self-supporting. Farmers on these holdings supplemented their incomes with other work. One man was a sheep-dip inspector, and another a gamekeeper and water bailiff – 'a job not highly respected in those days'. Joe's grandfather, who farmed one of the smallest holdings, also worked as a shoemaker. The farm that Joe inherited belonged to his uncle John, with whom Joe went to live when he was seven years of age.

People's accounts of their lives are always selective, and their reasons for including or excluding material are of course complex. The reference to political conflict in Gerry McCormick's account, for example, is unusual. In reviewing the testimonies used in this book it is noticeable that there is very little discussion of the communal divisions within Northern Ireland, which became world-famous in the 1970s. At first sight, this seems surprising. Many of the interviews were recorded during the 1980s, when the Ulster 'Troubles' were particularly bad, and people from all sections of Ulster society had their lives changed traumatically by violence, and the threat of it. These included some of the people whose testimonies provide the basis for this book.

Communal divisions within Ulster were not entirely ignored during interviews. Sometimes the issues described were relatively trivial. Pat McKillop, a north Antrim blacksmith, described an allegation made against himself, for example, that his sectarian allegiance led him to set plough irons differently for Catholics and Protestants preparing for a ploughing match. This was recounted with as much amusement as anger. On the other hand, competition for land, especially in areas where shifts in the sectarian balance of ownership were perceived as a possibility, could lead to long-term, bitter, and sometimes brutal feuds between families of different religious and political allegiances.

In general, however, people steered conversation away from divisive issues during interviews, and their reasons for doing so deserve respect. The field workers recording the interviews were themselves Northern Irish, and this have may have led to the use of what has been called 'a culture of avoidance', whereby people being interviewed deliberately steered conversation away from controversial topics with people who might possibly be involved in the local conflict. This way of dealing with life in Northern Ireland has sometimes been condemned as hindering 'real dialogue', but it can also be seen more positively, as a reluctance to offend or, more portentously, an attempt to keep the delicate social fabric of communication intact. Most people interviewed were anxious to emphasise that their neighbours did not fit into the hardened stereotypes of popular perception. The accounts of good relationships that were commonly given as evidence for this do seem to describe historical reality. In farm work, for example, it was often stated that neighbours would help one another irrespective of religious background, and the consistency of such testimonies suggests that this was more than a normative aspiration. In at least some areas, Protestant and Catholic neighbours maintained very friendly working and social relations.

The lack of emphasis on conflict also probably reflects people's view that their lives, and those of their neighbours, deserved celebration and affirmation; this may have led to a downplaying of more negative aspects of life. The values underlying this selective view of the past are valid, and the book attempts to respect the reticence of the people interviewed with regard to communal and other conflicts.

Many other events were selectively described or ignored in people's testimonies. We can sometimes attempt to identify the personal or social impulses behind particular instances of this kind of editing. Often, however, we can only recognise it as an ongoing possibility, which limits the extent to which we can accept accounts as rigorous and unbiased descriptions of the past.

The structure that people imposed on their testimonies also created distortion. The oral accounts were related as narratives, recounted in a meaningful sequence, which meant that information seen as unnecessary to the story, or that required qualification of the main theme, was often left out. Textual analysis is beyond the scope of this book, but it is important to bear in mind that the structuring of testimonies – and the shape given to them by what was forgotten, distorted, or deliberately repressed – creates refractions, making our task of clearly seeing the past very difficult. However, the past was there and is to some extent knowable, and the accounts, as well as the lived experience from which they were derived, bear witness to the value of the people's lives from which the historical account given in the following chapters is constructed.

2. Ulster farming
1930–1960

There are several big, bleak words that could be applied to Ulster farming since 1930. These include standardisation, centralisation, and mechanisation. This book aims to show how these movements impacted at the level of everyday life. Some of the negative impacts have been especially characteristic of the modern world: increasing alienation, deskilling, deepening social isolation, and the apparently inexorable rise of bureaucracy. However, it will also be shown that many changes in people's lives were dramatically enriching.

The idea that government had an obligation to support farming through education, grants, quality control, and statistical analysis was familiar to many Ulster farmers by the 1930s. Intervention had increased as a part of attempts to deal with a major depression in agriculture during the 1920s,[1] but had begun on a fairly large scale even earlier. The Irish Department of Agriculture and Technical Instruction, the Co-operative movement, and bodies such as the Congested Districts Board had made the notion of state intervention a familiar part of farming life from the earliest years of the twentieth century. In Northern Ireland, intervention moved to a new level during the 1920s, however, with radical measures such as the Egg Marketing Scheme of 1924. This scheme was important not only in counteracting – to some extent – the effects of competition from overseas, but also because it represented 'a pioneer movement within the United Kingdom in the compulsory marking and grading of agricultural produce'. Central planning developed further after 1930, based on the twin strategies of state protection and controlled marketing. Successful protection measures included the limitation of imports of frozen beef and lamb, processed milk and cream, potatoes, fat cattle, oats and eggs. In Northern Ireland, State marketing schemes, especially for pigs and milk, were also very effective. For example, the number of pigs per 1,000 acres more than doubled between 1933 and 1939. Direct financial aid was also very important, especially the subsidy for fat cattle other than cows. Exports of fat cattle to Britain more than doubled between 1933 and 1935, and remained at this level until 1939.[2]

Government intervention in quality control and marketing was particularly clear in the dairying industry. Much of the early intervention in this area seems to have been related to a world slump in prices during the 1930s. Before 1931, the Ministry of Agriculture in Northern Ireland had no direct control over milk processing. However, because of foreign competition, standardisation and control of exports came to be seen as desirable. In

December 1929, the Marketing of Dairy Produce Act (Northern Ireland) was passed, giving the Ministry complete control over creameries, butter factories and wholesale butter depots as from 1 January 1931. In 1934, this close supervision of the industry was matched by guaranteed prices. From 1 April in that year, an average price of 5d per gallon was paid in summer, and 6d per gallon in winter.[3]

The biggest single event leading to the entrenchment of government intervention in farming, however, was the Second World War. During the war, the Northern Irish Ministry of Agriculture followed Britain in introducing a compulsory tillage policy. Throughout Ireland, tillage had been in overall decline since around the Famine period of the 1840s; this was dramatically – albeit briefly – reversed during the war. Government policy, north and south, required farmers to increase crop production. In Northern Ireland, the acreage ploughed rose from 471,000 acres in 1939 to 851,000 acres in 1943.[4]

The British government urged farmers to increase production in dramatic, often bellicose language. In 1942, for example, the Ministry of Agriculture published the following, under the heading 'WHEAT IS A WAR WEAPON TO EVERY FARMER':

> Final victory depends on you as much as on the armed forces. Their job is to fight our battles: yours is to produce our food. Without food, battles cannot be won. Wheat is a vital source of food – BREAD. The nation's bread depends on you.
>
> SOW WHEAT AND SOW IT SOON[5]

The British government also exerted tight controls over agricultural labour supply, and even the purchase of machinery. In 1942, a directive stated that:

1. No agricultural tractor shall be sold or otherwise disposed of except with prior approval, in writing, from the Ministry.
2. No person shall acquire an agricultural tractor unless its sale or disposal to him has been approved by the Ministry, in writing.[6]

Government control extended even to the distribution of rubber boots. In 1944, farmers were told that 'The Ministry's allocation of permits for the purchase of rubber boots is now exhausted. No further applications can be considered until further notice.' An accompanying note explained that rubber supplies were extremely scarce, and most was allocated for use to the armed forces. Farmers 'lucky enough' to have tyres on tractors and carts were urged to take good care of them.[7]

In peacetime, directives such as these would appear dictatorial, but people living in rural areas during the war had a number of important advantages over townspeople. Some of these were illicit, notably the relative ease with which rationing restrictions could be bypassed. Mrs Mamie McQuoid of Kilmore in County Down related how, as a girl, she would be sent to neighbours to obtain extra butter:

> I used to have to go up to [a neighbour's farm] … for butter. And if you'd been caught getting butter you'd be in trouble, so I used to have to take the milk can with buttermilk [in it] and they would have put the pound of butter in the buttermilk, and that's how we got it home! … One night a policeman came down to tell us that our black-out blinds weren't pulled across properly – there was a wee bit of light showing – and mammy was trying to butter him up and make him tea, and she forgot herself and put a pound of country butter on the table … He didn't pass any remarks!

Ballynahinch Junction, where Mrs McQuoid lived, was easily reached from Belfast, and she said that people often came out from the city by train to buy eggs.

> People would come out … to the country to [buy eggs directly from farmers], and then the police would come, and they used to run round to my … mother's house, and leave the basket of eggs in the dining room, and then come out during the week [to get them]. Quite a lot [of people came] – Sunday was nearly always the night.

Some farmers also found ways around restrictions on animal feed. Mr James McKeown from Rademan, near Kilmore, remembered ways in which local farmers tried to get around the limits imposed by rationing on these items:

> The meal to the farmers was rationed as well, for the animals. But there was a wee man at Listooder … and there was two girls [who worked] in McRoberts' Mill … and when [this man] Tommy was going to order meal – you had to have your coupons with you to let them know what you were entitled to – he would have brought two bars of Cadbury's chocolate to give to the girls, and he would have got a bag or two extra thrown in! … There were certain meals – wheat meal and oatmeal – weren't rationed to farmers, you could have got as much of that as you wanted, but yellow meal or maize, or anything like that, it was rationed.[8]

At the legitimate, large-scale level of centralised planning, many aspects of government wartime controls also worked to the advantage of farmers, notably the guaranteed prices that were introduced at the same time as compulsory tillage. This kind of intervention occurred in many countries around the same time, and the expectation that governments would subsidise production became established throughout much of Europe.

By the 1950s, government policy was the single biggest factor in shaping farming, north and south. Rosemary Harris summed up the situation in the Ballygawley district of County Tyrone: 'In the 1950s it was most strikingly government agencies, especially the Ministry of Agriculture, that influenced the whole area through their implementation of the government's economic policies towards agriculture. By fixing prices and subsidies these agencies determined the relative attractiveness of different courses of action on the farms.'[9]

An emphasis on direct government intervention was a feature of economic planning in many countries during the post-war period. One massive consequence of this was the Common Agricultural Policy of the EEL, the dismantling of which has proved such a long-term and controversial task.

Wars are notoriously times when technological change speeds up, and this happened very dramatically during the Second World War. Mechanisation of farming accelerated greatly with the need for increased production, the shortage of labour, and government financial support. Flax-pulling machines multiplied with the short-term revival of flax growing,[10] milking machines were introduced to farms in increasing numbers,[11] and in 1944, the supply of self binders was insufficient to keep up with demand. There were 2,900 binders in Northern Ireland in 1939, and 5,800 by 1945.[12]

The spread of tractors was perhaps the most striking example of technological change. Tractors had been used in limited ways on Irish farms for most of the twentieth century (Fig. 7). Their use in farming during the 1930s had been greatly facilitated by Harry Ferguson's three-point linkage and hydraulic link, undoubtedly Ulster's greatest contribution to the development of international farming technology (Fig. 8). Ferguson was experimenting with his revolutionary system soon after the First World War, but commercial production began only in 1934, with the manufacture of Ferguson-Browns in Huddersfield, and even then this revolutionary development did not lead to the widespread use of tractors. Mr John A. Weir of Ballyroney, near Rathfriland, remembered the lack of enthusiasm for tractors shown by many farmers in the 1930s:

> I mind Ferguson and he had all the equipment in the Belfast Show, and it was over there to the left where you go into the horse jumping, and he was ploughing and making drills and everything, and there was hardly anybody stopping to look at it! … There was a man here, a neighbour of mine, and he had horses and they were giving him trouble putting in the crop, and he couldn't get them to work right. And he came down and asked me to ring up Ferguson's and ask them about the tractor and the implements. They said they would send a tractor and a lorry and all the implements, and men to demonstrate it, and if it wasn't entirely to his satisfaction as a customer they would take it away again, and it wouldn't cost him a ha'penny. And he didn't go on with it at that time [so it was wasted effort by Ferguson's]!

During the war, however, Ferguson's tractors were manufactured on a massive scale, and became an attractive investment for farmers benefiting not only from government support for crop production, but also from hire-purchase arrangements and special petrol allowances. Just before the war, in January 1939, there were only 550 tractors in Northern Ireland. By 1945, this had risen to 7,300.[13] In 1945, the Ministry of Agriculture reported that the number of tractors available was still inadequate to satisfy demand. However, 'It will be large enough if every farmer having horses makes the fullest use of them. If you have horses do as much ploughing and other work with them as possible and leave the tractor owners free to concentrate on ploughing for those who have no horses.'[14]

The changing attitudes to tractors can be seen clearly in the minutes of the Northern Ireland Ploughing Association (NIPA). In April 1939, The Association's Central Committee agreed that tractors would be included in the International Match organised for that year.[15] However, relations between the Ploughing Association and the newly

Fig. 7 Members of the McAlpine family harvesting wheat near Comber, County Down, c. 1939.
From left to right: Tom, Betty, James and David (L3812/9)

formed Tractor Users' Association (TUA) were obviously tense. A letter sent to the NIPA by the TUA in May 1939 stated the association's intention to organise a ploughing match for tractors, separate from the international match organised by the NIPA.[16] In July 1939, the issue was discussed at the Central Committee meeting of the NIPA. Following a walk-out by the tractor men, one ploughman put forward a motion 'that we have nothing to do with tractors'.[17] This motion was withdrawn after discussion, and tractors were included in the 1939 match. The 1940 match was not held because of the war, and when the issue was discussed in 1943, one member of the committee stated that he was 'not in favour of tractors at all … Mr Campbell raised the point of getting a field big enough for horses, let alone tractors as well.'[18] By 1945, however, the Association's Secretary reported the possibility that there would be more prizes for tractors than horses at the international match that year.[19]

After the war, the number of working horses in Northern Ireland (74,770) was roughly the same as in 1939 (75,560),[20] and numerically, tractors still made little impact. In the Inishmore district of Fermanagh in 1947, for example, only three farmers out of 127 included in a survey had tractors; even in the Braid Valley in County Antrim, known for its commercial farming, tractors were owned by only three farmers out of 72.[21] The end of the working horse was in sight, however. In 1944, a Ministry of Agriculture report from

Cavanreagh, near Draperstown, described the situation on the farm of Mr John Sinclair very enthusiastically, clearly seeing this as the way forward:

> Mr Sinclair is one of those enthusiastic farmers who believes in adopting labour-saving devices whenever practicable … For instance, he has harnessed a water wheel in the farmyard to drive a barn thresher, a set of fans for cleaning corn, a corn crusher, a turnip pulper, a circular saw and a dynamo for making electric light. Electric light is installed in the dwelling house and farm buildings. Again, the work of the farm has been mechanised since 1940 when a Ford-Ferguson was purchased and Mr Sinclair soon saw that the tractor, used with discretion, could entirely replace horses for all types of farm work. There are now no horses on the farm.[22]

The rate at which tractors overtook horses varied markedly throughout Ulster. As late as 1957, 49% of tractors in Northern Ireland were found in Antrim and Down; around this time, the overall number of tractors exceeded the number of horses for the first time.[23]

The Sinclair farm just mentioned was also in the forefront of the 'quiet revolution' created by the spread of electric power to farming. As with tractors, the spread of electricity was uneven. Many farms were not supplied with mains electricity before the late 1940s and the 1950s. In 1947, only 1,738 farms in Northern Ireland had electric power. After 1954, however, an average of over 2,000 farms were connected each year, and by the end of 1960 over 23,000 farms were connected – almost one-third of the farms in Northern Ireland.[24]

Mr Robert Strain described the process of electrification in the Rathfriland district of County Down. A private company initially supplied the town with electric light.

> It was owned by a gentleman called Finney, who also had a private plant in Banbridge … In the 1930s [these plants] would have been [powered by] diesel … There was a pretty crude system around the houses … [The wires] would all have been above ground, on poles and then house to house they would simply have been clipped along under the gutter. The nearest that electricity came to us was in 1945, it came to Weir's [foundry] in Ballyroney … Up to that, he had been running the works with a 32 horse [power] Blackstone diesel engine …
>
> The main line to Rathfriland, to bring the power there, came from Banbridge … and there was a spur came off it to supply Weir. And at the same time as it supplied him, there were seven or eight different properties near him got it. In fact one of the places was Ballyroney Presbyterian Church … That was in 1945 …
>
> Very few farms had a private supply of electricity. One man … James Quinn Morrison, he had an engine, dynamo and a bank of batteries … That gave you light but no power … Any farm that was a bit more advanced and got a milking machine, had to buy a small engine to drive it. [Usually a Lister using petrol.]
>
> [Around Rathfriland] the first move [towards extending electrification] into the rural areas came in the 1950s … They used 11,000 [voltage] road lines … and they would have supplied about five kilowatts through a transformer, which they reckoned would have been sufficient to deal with most farms … There was very little use of machinery [in farms, however] … The electricity came to my own home in 1955 … [There] was great excitement when it came of course … Apart from lights in the house, the one thing a lot

Fig. 8 A Ferguson tractor ploughing in the 1930s (photograph courtesy of the Museum of English Rural Life)

of people got was an electric cooker … The odd person would have bought, usually, a small one horse motor on the milking machine. Indeed in my own case at home, we put a small one horse motor on a pump … and used it to pump water [from the well] into a tank in the roof space, because there was no mains water.

I don't think [electricity] … had much effect on the efficiency of farming … it was an improvement from the point of view of living conditions mostly.

Mrs Mamie McQuoid of Kilmore, County Down, confirmed the labour-saving blessings of electricity. One major advantage for women was their release from having to look after oil lamps, and another was the vacuum cleaner, which Mrs McQuoid got in 1952. A further boon for many women was the electric smoothing iron, which made ironing clothes much less back-breaking. In the same area of County Down, Mr James McKeown's experience echoed that of Mr Robert Strain, just quoted. The McKeowns got electric power on their farm at Rademan in 1951, but apart from its use for milking machines, it had little early application in farming.

Fig. 9 Mr William Boyce of Broughshane, County Antrim demonstrating how to pack eggs in 1951 (L2962/11)

3. Farm produce

Throughout Ulster, mixed farming has been the norm, but since the Great Famine of the 1840s there has been an increasing emphasis on livestock farming. By 1939, 80% of farm output in Northern Ireland came from livestock and livestock products. This was sharply reversed during the Second World War, when the acreage under tillage almost doubled, but the trend reversed again after 1945 and by 1957, 91.3% of the gross output of farming in Northern Ireland came from livestock. Most of this output was from cattle, pigs and poultry (Fig. 9).

Product	% of gross output
Beef cattle	27.3
Pigs	25
Poultry	23.5
Milk	20.5
Sheep	4
Total	100

Note: 75% of the gross value of crops grown at this time came from potatoes.[1]

Dairying, pig farming and poultry farming require a lot of capital investment; the scale of investment required for dairying meant that this was not practised on most very small farms.[2]

In some ways, diversification suited the small size of most Ulster farms very well. On a small farm, where land area was limited, it was argued that diversification allowed the fullest use of family labour, as tasks associated with the various elements of production involved different levels of work, at different times during the year. It also meant that uncertainty of income could be reduced, as at any time it was likely that some commodities would do well and others not so well. Diversification also meant that sources of income were spread more evenly throughout the year; for example, the sale of pigs would take place at different times from peak milk production. After the war, however, there was concern that the lack of specialisation on small farms could lead to inefficiency, as farmers often could not keep abreast of technical developments. A varied production pattern tended to make investment in specialised machinery relatively uneconomic, as a mixed farm would require a wide range of machines.[3]

Fig. 10 Preparing ground for vegetables near Ballygowan, County Down, in 1953

Specialisation, such as it was, was confined to a small number of districts (Fig. 10):

> There are a few areas which have specialised to a greater or lesser degree on particular
> crops. Such are the hill slopes on either side of the Lagan valley producing milk for sale
> in Belfast; the floor of that valley and the area around Newtownards are devoted to market
> gardening; in Lurgan and district poultry and eggs are very important; the northern part
> of Co. Armagh has many apple orchards, and the growing of bush fruits is beginning here;
> Down produces half of the ryegrass seed.[4]

However, in general, as the following six case studies show, variations in patterns of farming
related more to scale, methods employed and the farm's location than to specialised types
of farming. The examples chosen are an arbitrary sample, and many other patterns and
associated strategies could be documented. The intention is to illustrate some of the key
differences between small, medium and large holdings.

The Murphy family

This medium-sized family farm was on the edge of the Mourne mountains, County Down;
rugged hill country that has been known as a sheep-farming area since at least the mid-
nineteenth century. The Murphy family farmed land in the townland of Mullaghmore near
Hilltown from the early 1700s, when it was rented from the Marquis of Downshire. Patrick

Fig. 11 Frank and John Murphy in the farmyard at Hilltown, County Down, in 1929 (L2728/11)

Murphy bought the farm in 1919, and after his death in 1937 his sons continued working on it until 1976.

Patrick married twice. His first wife gave birth to two sons, who emigrated to California in 1910. Mary Catherine Murphy, his second wife, had a much larger family of six sons and five daughters. She died in 1946. The farm at Mullaghmore, or 'the Glen' as the area is known locally, included some good arable land, and about fifty acres of mountain. It was bigger than most farms in the area, three-quarters of these being less than 30 acres.[5] The farmyard had a solid two-storey stone house, backed by an enclosed yard, containing a byre with a hay loft above, outhouses for pigs and cattle, and sheds for farm equipment (Fig. 11). In 1937, after Patrick Murphy's death, his sons made a haggard adjoining the yard.

Peter Owen Murphy, one of the brothers active in running the farm from the 1920s onwards, said that in a typical year during the 1930s about three acres of potatoes were grown, usually 'blues' of the Arran Banner variety, or in later years, Kerr's Pinks (Fig. 12). About seven acres of oats were grown as animal fodder, along with four or five acres of hay and an acre of turnips.

Throughout the Second World War years flax was grown on the farm – three acres of it in 1945, when it was then taken to a local scutch mill. A classic study of farming in Northern Ireland, published in 1947, described the operation of these mills in the Hilltown district:

The flax is taken from a stack or store at the mill, generally by the farmer who owns the crop. It then passes through a series of corrugated rollers … Emerging from the rollers this flax is made up into handfuls or stricks by a woman or boy. Armfuls of these stricks are passed on to the scutcher. Scutching consists of holding the stricks of flax against a rotating fan. This fan is composed of a series of beechwood arms attached to a rotating wheel. The woody matter breaks up into tiny chips and dust known as shaws. The atmosphere in any scutchmill is so thick with this dust that it is often difficult to see the scutchers. One tiny stream of clean air from outside the mill is brought in by the beaters and the scutcher puts his nose in this. It takes two men to remove all the shaws, a buffing man and a cleaner … Normal output is about 8 stone per day, but this varies a good deal, as flax is a notoriously chancy crop and some yields much better than others. Hence the reason for each farmer attending the scutching of his own flax.[6]

The Murphy family had an arrangement with the local mill in Hilltown where they worked at scutching their own flax. Local farmers tried to time the readiness of their flax for scutching so that neighbours would not require the use of the mill at the same time. Peter Owen Murphy described the arrangement.

One [local] man had his flax in the mill [on the] 15th August … He had sowed early … Our flax would be scutched about November … That's when [the other] crop would be all out … When the spuds were dug, the [retted] flax [which had been stored in two stacks on the farm] was sent to the mill … We worked in the mill … [Paid workers had two shifts]. They worked from eight o'clock in the morning till about two. Then the other crowd came on and worked from two o'clock till about half past twelve at night … I done it many a time … just when our own flax was doing – just three or four days of it.

Fig. 12 Planting potatoes at Hilltown, 2 May 1931. From left to right: Joey, John, Frank and Peter Owen Murphy, and their cousin Peter McConville (L2728/2)

The scutched flax was sold in Rathfriland, where flax markets were held on Wednesdays. Buyers from large spinning mills purchased the fibre: Cowdy's of Banbridge, Ewart's of Belfast, and Richardson's of Bessbrook.

Changes in the technology used to cultivate crops on the Murphy's farm were similar to those made on many medium-sized Ulster farms during the twentieth century. Until the late 1940s, three horses were usually kept on the farm – two draught horses and 'a small mare for going in the trap'. Like many people in the Hilltown area, the Murphys often bought horses at the spring fair in Camlough, south Armagh. Horses had a working life of about ten years, after which they were changed. In the early decades of this century a swing plough was used on the farm, but in 1925 a wheel or 'chill' plough was purchased. A neighbour of the Murphys bought the first tractor in the Glen area in 1945. The family bought their own Ferguson tractor in 1947, and the last horse was sold in 1949.

There was a horse-operated threshing machine on the Murphy's farm. When it broke down around 1918, the family began to hire a portable thresher from Mayobridge. The machine was powered by a steam engine until the mid-1940s, when tractor power became available. The farm's harvested grain crop was usually built into about ten stacks. Before the haggard, or stack yard, was made, the stacks were built across the 'headland' of a field, and threshing was usually carried out there.

During the period the Murphy children were at home, six Shorthorn cows were kept on the farm. Most members of the family helped with milking, and the initial churning of butter, for which most of the milk was used. Much of the butter was used at home, but some was also sold to a grocery shop in Hilltown. After Mrs Mary Catherine Murphy's death, when most of the family had left the farm, only two cows were kept, and the large dash churn was replaced by a 'wee tumblin' churn' in which butter was made for home use.

A sow was kept on the farm, and litters of piglets were produced from her, to be sold after weaning. The family also sometimes had a pig slaughtered for home use. Two local butchers did the killing, and the Murphys then cured the bacon and ham, as well as eating the liver and 'puddins'. Mary Catherine Murphy had 'a yard full of hens', and also reared turkeys and ducks, but the main livestock kept on the farm were sheep (Fig. 13). Patrick Murphy kept about seventy ewes, his sons later increasing this number to around ninety. The reliance on sheep was uncommon on Ulster farms of the period, and was largely due to the proximity of the Mourne mountains, where there was abundant common grazing. In the Hilltown area, however, a limit was placed on the number of sheep that could be put on the mountain. A report produced in the early 1960s stated that:

> the Mournes are practically all common mountain … A small head-rate is charged on each sheep grazed (usually sixpence or one shilling) but there is no limit to the numbers that can be put on except for the area west of Hilltown … [including the townland of] Mullaghmore … where the maximum for each tenant is 65 … On the Hilltown ridge the main enterprise is the breeding of foundation ewe stock. The ewes produce lambs for 2 to 3 years and are then sold to farmers further north at the autumn fairs at Hilltown.[7]

Fig. 13 Frank, John and Joey Murphy with mountain rams due to be sold at the Tip Fair in Hilltown, in October 1930 (L2728/8)

The Murphys sheared their own sheep around the end of June. Using handclippers, a sheep could be shorn in about ten minutes. The fleeces were then baled up and sold to a buyer in Hilltown. There were three sheep fairs held in Hilltown each year, in August, September, and October, for the sale of lambs.

Peter Owen Murphy preferred the local 'Mourne' sheep to 'Scotch' blackface:

> Frank [my brother] bought two Scotch tips [rams] in Belfast … He always went down there and bought tips … [But the problem was,] them tips were housed all winter … An oul' tip, he stayed a while here, and he died out in the field. A bad buy them oul' tips away down in Belfast … Our [Mourne] tips are bigger, standing up far bigger. The Scotch tips are small … [they] don't stand up high enough …
>
> Mourne sheep are good for breeding. [They're] mostly speckled-faced sheep. You don't want an oul' dark-faced sheep … you want … good long legs on them - good props. The oul' fellow used to say, 'Why do you want a wee sheep with short legs?' … The Mourne sheep were better sheep – they're a hardier breed.

Peter's views on the superiority of Mourne sheep were upheld by at least one researcher in the 1960s, who agreed that 'pure-bred Mourne Blackface … are best suited to conditions on the mountain grazings'.[8]

The McSparran family

The Glens of Antrim, which run from the Antrim hills into the Irish Sea, combine hill country, a spectacular coastline, and limited amounts of good land on valley floors. The

McSparran farmhouse and yard are situated on this low-lying land, in the townland of Cloney, near Cushendun. Malachy McSparran said that records preserved in old notebooks suggest that farming was not carried on very intensively in his grandfather's time, but the pattern established was developed by his father. Under his grandfather's management, young cattle were bought and fattened and a few cows were milked for family use.

Archibald McSparran, Malachy's father, increased the scale of this activity. The maximum acreages remembered by Malachy McSparran were harvested during the Second World War: seven acres of flax, fifteen acres of oats, three or four acres of potatoes, an acre of turnips. One year three acres of barley were also grown.

Malachy's father would often buy between forty and fifty store cattle, which were put on hill pasture for the summer, and mostly sold at the 'back end' of the year. Those not sold were stall-fed and later sold as beef cattle. Six or seven cows, mostly Shorthorns, were hand-milked, and until 1960 this milk was sold to a local creamery, although Malachy's mother also made some into butter for family use. A Galloway bull was usually kept on the farm. Galloway cattle were common in the Glens of Antrim. They were kept because they could 'lie out' all winter. Malachy said that the cross between a Galloway bull and a Shorthorn cow produced a 'very good, hardy type of cattle'. During the 1950s Friesian cattle began to be introduced, and in 1956 Malachy McSparran bought a Hereford bull. 'I remember the people of the country looking at it with amazement. They thought it was a terrible big head!'

Archibald McSparran kept between 120 and 130 sheep, only about a quarter of the number now kept on the farm. Most of the sheep were a cross between Blackface ewes and a Border Leicester ram. Wool from the sheep was sold, but they were mainly valued for their lambs, which were sold as stores to a buyer who came to the area around the end of August each year. This man resold the lambs to lowland farmers who either fattened them for slaughter or kept them as replacements in their permanent flocks.

Between four and five sows were kept on the farm, and the piglets they produced were usually sold as 'weaners' at around eleven or twelve weeks of age, although occasionally pigs were fattened before selling. A local man killed pigs for the McSparrans, especially during the Second World War, and these were cured for family use.

Women in the McSparran family kept large numbers of hens (Fig. 14). After the Second World War Malachy's mother converted a barn into a deep litter house. Up to two crates, each holding thirty dozen eggs, were sold every week to an egg merchant in Cushendall.

Horses were kept in large numbers on the farm. Malachy described his father's system:

> He would have about … fifteen or sixteen young foals and kept them all winter, and then in the spring of the year he would have sold them as 'clibs' … The local people would have bought them and broken them in and used them … There was a foal fair at Glenariffe on the first of November, and he would often have bought foals there, or [at] Cushendall, or even bought them locally … He knew if somebody had a foal, and would have gone and bought them … They would have been the ordinary type of working horse you have here – there would be some … Cushendall type of ponies in it … [but] I would say Irish Draught would have been the main breed.

The McSparrans also usually kept three working horses. They bought the first wheel plough in their area in the 1920s, and neighbours gathered to see what was then considered a technological novelty. (In many parts of the Glens of Antrim, swing ploughs were used until they were replaced by tractor ploughs.) The family bought their first tractor in 1941, but a horse was also kept for several years afterwards.

The Wilson family

The Wilson family farm was in Townavanney, a townland on the northern shore of Lower Lough Erne, facing Boa island. The nearest small towns were Kesh, about eight miles to the east, and Belleek, about eleven miles to the west. Mary Wilson went to live on the farm after her marriage in October 1937. Her husband, Thomas Wilson, had a farm of forty-two acres of fairly good land, and common grazing in a 'mountain' area of about one hundred and thirty acres, which he shared with four other farmers. The Wilson family cut turf on Derrin mountain, about one and a half miles from the farm (Fig. 15).

The crops grown on the farm in the late 1930s were oats (7 acres), potatoes (3 acres), barley (3 acres), turnips ($^1/_2$ acre), and hay. Potatoes and carrots were grown in a small vegetable garden, where there were also several apple trees. Until 1962, when the family bought a tractor, the heavy work of cultivation was carried out using horses. Most of the crops were used as fodder for the farm's livestock. Dairy cattle and pigs were the main source of income. In the 1930s and 1940s about ten cows were kept, and each year between eight and ten calves were born on the farm. Some of the calves were kept as stores, to replace old cows. Most, however, were sold at fairs in Belleek, or Pettigo, a village some six miles away. Calves were usually sold when they were about one and a half years old. The family preferred to sell them during spring, but sometimes kept them till early autumn. Most calves were bought by dealers, who often sent them by rail to Derry, and then shipped them to England and Scotland. Until Mr Thomas Wilson retired at the age of sixty-five, all milking on the farm was done by hand. His son Trevor introduced milking machines soon after taking over the farm. Some milk was skimmed and kept to feed calves and pigs, the cream being made into butter. Milk was also sold to a creamery in Kesh, every day in summer and on Mondays, Thursdays and Saturdays in winter. The family received a 'milk cheque' from the creamery once a month, and the creamery also gave back the skimmed milk left after the cream had been removed from the farm's milk.

At one time seven sows were kept on the farm, mostly of the Large White Ulster and Wessex breeds. These produced forty to fifty young pigs a year. Their usual feed was boiled potatoes mixed with oatmeal, Indian meal or a little bran, supplemented by skimmed milk. The Wilsons hired the services of a boar on a farm several miles away, their sows being brought there by horse and cart. At any time, two of the sows might have litters of piglets, and often three litters were produced within a month. The piglets were left with the sow for eight to ten weeks, and after this were moved to a different house where they were fed on 'roughage'. After six months the young pigs were sold.

Fig. 14 Malachy McSparran's grandmother, Dora McArdle, feeding hens at her farm in Mullaghduff, Cullyhanna, County Armagh. Malachy's aunt Annie McArdle is in the background (L3066/6)

Fig. 15 Bringing home the turf at the Wilsons' farm at Townavanney, County Fermanagh. Thomas Wilson is on the right, along with two neighbour girls and his nephew from Newry, County Down (2727/5)

Until the late 1950s a local butcher slaughtered pigs intended for sale on the family farm. Up to twelve pigs might be killed on one day. Like many country people, Mrs Wilson found the slaughtering upsetting, and avoided it. After killing, the hair on the hide was scraped off, and the carcass was scalded. The innards were removed after the pigs had been hung up. Two days later the carcasses were sold to a travelling dealer from Enniskillen. After the home slaughtering of pigs for market stopped, live animals were usually sent by lorry to Derry, in return for payment at an agreed rate, by cheque.

Pigs were also slaughtered on the farm for home use. In this case the carcass was particularly carefully washed, and hung up for four or five days. It was then cut up in pieces, which were rubbed with salt. The pieces were tightly packed in a tub, and weighted boards were put on top of the tub to compress the pork. After three weeks, the meat could be removed as needed. Meat that was properly stored could remain in good condition for up to a year. Each piece of bacon or ham was soaked overnight before cooking, to remove salt. Hams were a delicacy reserved for visitors, while bacon was for everyday use. The only piece of the innards used as food was the liver. The rest of the offal was taken away and buried. On a day when a number of pigs were slaughtered for market, Mrs Wilson sent some of the livers to neighbours, who did the same when pigs were being slaughtered on their own farms.

Mr Thomas Wilson kept about seven ewes on the farm, mostly of the Suffolk and Border Leicester breeds. Mrs Wilson's father had kept sheep, near Pettigo in County Fermanagh, but Mrs Wilson said these were mostly on an outlying farm rather than the main family holding. On both farms the sheep were kept mainly for their lambs, which were sold at nearby fairs and markets to butchers, or farmers who wanted to rear them for breeding. There was also a thriving market for woollen fleeces, however. The hand-clipped fleeces from the Wilson's farm were sold to an agent in Kesh.

Mrs Wilson looked after a flock of up to one hundred and fifty hens, mostly of Leghorn, Wyandotte and Sussex varieties. She reared up to two hundred chicks in a year. When she came to the farm in 1937, eggs were put under brooding hens, but just after the Second World War she bought a brooder, which was a suitably heated device in which newly hatched chicks could be reared. This, together with day old chicks, was supplied by Farbairn's hatcheries, Portadown. Most eggs from the farm's hens were sold to a travelling grocer who came to the farm once a week, and the cash earned was used to buy groceries such as tea, sugar, bread, jam and butter. The 'egg money' was a useful extra for the family budget.

The Kane family

County Fermanagh is celebrated for its maze of lakeland, wooded islands, and low but dramatic limestone hills. The quality of the land varies greatly within the county, but in many parts there is an ongoing struggle to maintain drainage. Around Ederney, in the north-west of the county, land can quickly revert to rushes if left for even a few years. Joe Kane lived with his uncle on a very small holding in Drumkeeran in this part of the county. The main crops grown on the farm were potatoes, hay and oats. Almost all of the tillage work was carried out using spades, and a very complex system of ridge and furrow cultivation. Potatoes were grown in the same ground for two consecutive years, after which the land was used for hay and oats. During the Second World War, when cultivation was most extended, about two acres of potatoes, three and a half acres of hay, and an acre of oats were grown. Joe Kane was a keen gardener. He regularly cultivated a wide variety of vegetables, including beans, peas, onions, shallots, parsnips, carrots and garlic. In the past, cabbages were set along the sides of potato ridges, at intervals of about two and a half paces apart.

The most important livestock on the farm were cattle and pigs, but often only one of each was kept. A single horse was also kept, but at infrequent intervals (Fig. 16).

> Sometimes this man [his uncle] was very poor – he hadn't a big lot of animals … He used to keep two cows and a pony one time … When the pony got old he kept the cows on, and then the cows, one after the other, they got old, and he wasn't able to replace them … there was some times he only had one cow and we often had to do without the milk.

The other product of the cow that was of great importance on the farm was manure, both for the potato crop and for top-dressing meadows.

Fig. 16 Joe Kane with a young horse at Drumkeeran, County Fermanagh, in the 1930s (L2727/3)

The pig kept on the farm was usually of either the Large White Ulster or the York breed. It was fed on boiled potatoes, meal, scraps, and 'a sup of sweet milk' when this was available. The pig was usually bought when it was about six weeks old, and fattened until it weighed between a hundredweight and a quarter and a hundredweight and a half.

If it was allowed to grow heavier, Joe Kane said that it would not fetch so much money at market. For many years a local man, Johnny Lyttle, killed pigs on the farm. This man had no formal veterinary training but was greatly admired for his ability to tend sick animals. He usually castrated young pigs, which in itself was very low paid work, but Joe Kane said that it was accepted that the man who castrated the young pigs was also given the task of slaughtering them, a much better paid job.

After killing, scalding, and the cleaning out of innards, the pig was hung for a day before being brought to Irvinestown market. The liver and heart were kept for use at home. Neighbours who had more than one pig being slaughtered would sometimes send a liver to the Kanes, and other neighbours. The pig carcass was an important source of cash for rent to the local landlord before 1926, and after this for payments made to the state towards buying out the holding.

Joe and his uncle kept few poultry. At one time Joe kept only one hen and one cockerel, but he did make some money from poultry by collecting eggs from neighbours using his own donkey and cart. This was during the Second World War when lorries did not run because of frequent petrol shortages.

The Ward family

West Donegal has an Atlantic landscape of great beaches, rugged headlands, and rocky ground, much of which is covered by blanket bog. Hugh Paddy Óg Ward was born in 1910, one of eight children reared on a farm typical of many in this western area, the Rosses (Fig. 17). The farm, situated in Keadew townland about three miles north of Burtonport, had seven acres of arable land, and rights to common grazing on a sea meadow of eighteen acres which was jointly controlled by four families. All of the arable land was periodically cultivated, but the farm's produce was not sufficient to maintain the family. The Wards, like most families in the Rosses and neighbouring Gweedore, supplemented their income by activities other than farming, and particularly by migrant labour.

Spades were the most important tillage implements on the farm. Partly this was made economical by the small size of the holding, but spadework was also the tillage technique best suited to the uneven rocky ground. Hugh Ward said that until the recent past most of the cultivated land in the area had been covered by a layer of blanket bog, which was slowly removed by turf cutting. Bog to the north of Keadew strand was still being cut when he was a boy. The last of the bog had been cleared from the Wards' farm when Hugh's father was a young man. A large rock behind the family house now stands about six feet above the surrounding land. Hugh's father could remember spades striking the top of this rock when the bog covering it was cleared.

A bewildering range of spadework techniques is used or remembered throughout Ireland, but the main technique used on the Wards' farm, known locally as 'delving', was similar to the 'improved' method of trenching frequently described in early agricultural textbooks.[9] Delving was a necessary first step in preparing ground for potato drills, another 'improved' method which, Hugh Ward says, became widely used in Donegal during his own boyhood.

The Ward family planted about a ton of potato seed each year, for both human consumption and animal fodder. New seed was purchased every few years from the 'Board', or the Department of Agriculture. Most years, however, small potatoes were saved from the harvested crop to provide seed.

Fig. 17 Hugh Ward in his garden at Keadew in west Donegal, in 1987

Potatoes require large amounts of fertiliser. On the Wards' farm the main source of manure was animal dung, but the farm's coastal location meant that seaweed was also available. When Hugh Ward was very young, each farming family had its own area of shore from which seaweed (known locally as *leathach* or 'wrack') was cut. In the 1980s, wrack was still cut and sold to a processing plant in the nearby town of Dungloe, but seaweed was also spread on the fields. Most seaweed was cut from rocks at low tide, using hooks. Cutting could take place at a considerable distance from the land, and the seaweed was brought ashore in boats, usually yawls about twenty feet in length.

> I only mind once being out with my father … shifting a cargo of wrack, you know … [I was about twelve years old] and it was me that steered the boat. I was on the helm … and they were pulling with two oars … and there wasn't [two inches] … left over the water … only it was quite calm … We were up near Burtonport … There's a place there called Roshin … and you went down the road with your horse and cart … and there was a little pier [where] … they landed the wrack. [Back on the farm] … it was dumped along the road … and you would get a barrel … and you put your creel sitting on that, and you filled the creel with the graip, and put it out in creelfuls all along the drills.

Hugh said that although soil on the farm was often shallow and hard to dig, yields were good – about ten tons of potatoes to the acre. The rich lands of the Laggan in east Donegal yielded about eighteen tons to the acre, but Hugh also remembered working on a farm in northern England where the yield was only eight tons.

After potatoes, oats were the most important crop grown on the farm. Oats were sown by hand in mid-April and could be ready to harvest by mid-August, scythes being the main harvest implement used. The crop was usually sufficient to make five stacks, which yielded about forty stones of grain after threshing using flails. Hugh's father brought the grain to a mill in Dungloe, receiving half of it back as ground oatmeal, which was used to make a strongly flavoured type of porridge, a favourite bedtime meal with older men. The oat straw was used as fodder for cattle.

Hay was also used for fodder. About half an acre was sown with grass-seed for two consecutive years, on ground that the family believed was in danger of becoming over-cropped. After mowing, haymaking was carried on using forks and rakes. The hay was built first into small heaps known as 'rucks', which were later put together in larger rucks. The dried hay was carted to the 'stack garden' beside the house. In very wet weather, hay spread on the ground was made into small rolls, known as 'laps' or 'granigs' (from the Irish, *gráinneog*).

During winter the cattle were fed on hay and oat straw. Milking cattle were given extra feed, potatoes with Indian meal on top and boiling water poured over them.

Young cattle were given some bran and turnips. Calves did not suckle the cows. The cows were milked by hand morning and evening, and at these times the calves were given some milk in a bucket or dish. The calves were sold at a fair held in Dungloe during the month of May, and were a valuable source of income, especially at a time of year when little money could be expected from the sale of crops or from the earnings of migrant labourers.

Donkeys were common in Keadew. Hugh Ward remembered strings of forty to fifty donkeys crossing the strand loaded with creels of turf. Up to the outbreak of the Second World War, however, Hugh's father kept a horse and cart, which he used to supplement family income. At some times during the year he would be working every day with the cart, transporting goods landed at Burtonport to places such as Dungloe or the northern village of Annagry. An average wage would have been around seven shillings for the day, but if turf was being moved, meals would also be provided during the day.

Hugh's father kept six ewes on the sea meadow grazing area. A sluice has now been installed for drainage, and a Gaelic football pitch now occupies part of the land, but when used for grazing, the meadows had been regularly flooded at high tide. Hugh claimed that the salt water ensured the good quality of the grass. Each year the ewes would produce up to twelve lambs, and these were bought by a local butcher, who declared them to be twice as good as lambs he bought from anywhere else.

The Drennans of Carse Hall

During the first half of the nineteenth century, the eastern shores of Lough Foyle became one of the richest farming areas in Ulster. The development happened in a very short time. At the start of the century, the area was described as an 'ouzy marsh'.[10] Between 1838 and 1851, however, the coastal flats were reclaimed, and the construction of embankments, drainage channels and pumping houses transformed the area from ill-drained slobland to farmland with rich alluvial soils up to two feet in depth. The new land was laid out in large farms, one of these being Carse Hall. This account of farming at Carse Hall is largely based on the testimony of the late Mr John C. Drennan, but there is also an unusually large amount of documentation available to study the history of the farm. When it was sold in 1958, the Drennan family deposited farm papers in the Public Record Office of Northern Ireland.[11]

Oral and written testimonies agree that James Drennan of Ayrshire bought the farm in 1855.[12] It was a huge farm by Irish standards, consisting of 640 acres, all arable land. This made it one of the wealthiest farms in Ulster. The scale of operations on the farm reflected its wealth. A Clydesdale stud company was established in the 1880s, and by the early twentieth century this had become the largest of its kind in Ireland (Fig. 18). John C. Drennan also believed that the farm was one of the few in Ireland where steam power was applied to farming operations such as tillage in the nineteenth century. The most successful investment in steam power was made by his father, who purchased five steam threshing complexes that were hired out to farms in the area.

John C. Drennan took over the running of the farm on the death of his father in 1916, and he farmed it until it was sold in 1958. Its range of buildings indicates the complexity of the operation. The farmyard had pens in which a hundred cattle were fattened, and stalls for fifteen horses. There were also cart sheds, and sheds for hay and straw. These were not big enough to store all of the farm's harvest, so a large 'stack garden' was used, which held

Fig. 18 John C. Drennan showing a Clydesdale at the North West of Ireland Agricultural Society's Summer Show in the Brandywell (photograph courtesy of Mr T. MacDonald and Mr D. Bigger)

up to sixty stacks. The stack garden was a well-known landmark for rail travellers. '[It] used to be quite famous, because every stack was built to an absolute inch of height … They were all finished the same way, and after that they were thatched, they were all clipped … the train ran through the centre of my farm – the line from Derry to Belfast'.

Other buildings provided space for specialised functions, including the dairy, forge, harness room, and a pumping station.

> The main thing about this farm was that we had to pump all the water which fell on the farm. It was all drained up to a pump house. In [early days] … it was all done by steam – two big centrifugal pumps … In 1932 we got the Electricity Board to put a line down to the pumping station, and we use[d] electricity … from 1932 onwards … The engine [only ran] in mid-winter. I remember one occasion she never stopped day and night for three weeks … because of a very wet season … and the bank broke at that time.

Carse Hall was not the only dwelling on the farm. Farm workers lived in cottages that were part of the main building complex, two being in the farmyard and six in a row nearby. Another two 'semi-detached' cottages were set at right angles to this row.

Most of the crops grown on the farm were used as fodder for livestock. In the early twentieth century about three hundred acres were kept in grass. Up to forty acres of turnips were cultivated, and beans were also grown, dried and ground on the farm. Sufficient hay and oats were produced to fill the sheds and the stack garden.

The Drennans bought an International Harvester tractor very early, in 1916, but for several decades horses remained the most important source of power for crop cultivation. Before the Second World War, eleven working horses were kept, 'five and a half pair'. Most horses on the farm were part of the stud business, and the best of these were sent to shows such as the Royal Ulster Agricultural Show, held at Balmoral in Belfast. Some of the horses were kept only for a short time before being sold. The stud stallion was usually changed every three years. When John Drennan took over the farm, the basic stock of the stud was five Clydesdale mares and a stallion.

> You'd only keep a stallion for about three years, because his fillies would be coming back again … at that time, so you'd to get another to serve those fillies … We kept on doing that, and then I started taking up the show business, and really got interested in horses … I increased the stud. At one time I had ten brood mares. I had nine foals one year … We used a lot of the arable part for grazing the mares and foals … Then as well as that I imported a lot of animals, females mostly, to sell to people about here. We had a sale for a big number of years … every second year … The farmers round about wanted females to breed off … I would say that I could put anything from one hundred horses through my hands every year.

Sheep and cattle were also kept on the farm. Around one hundred and thirty beef cattle were grazed each summer, and one hundred bullocks were housed each winter. The management of cattle and sheep was closely interlinked.

> For … quite a few years I used to breed sheep, but I found very often that when it came to lambing time, my shepherd seemed to be off sick and I had to do the lambing, so I stopped that. I always had about one hundred and fifty ewes … [so] it was a job … lambing [them].
>
> Latterly, I used to winter cattle outside, [but] I discovered after several years that I couldn't get the early grass, which was the time you could buy cattle to make some money … So I stopped wintering cattle outside, and started … [to] buy cross-bred lambs from round the hills here … and in the winter time we just used to let those lambs run all over the farm so that they could clean up the grass and so on, with the result that in the spring of the year, after you put a good touch of fertiliser [on the ground] you could get good early grass, and we could buy cattle much earlier, with the result that [we] could buy them cheaper.

John Drennan's mother kept a pig, but 'that was her own property … [it] wasn't part of the farm at all, it was there for [a] specific purpose, to use up the swill of the house'.

Farming methods

The general size of farms in Ulster is small. In 1937, 38% of all holdings in Northern Ireland were under fifteen acres, and 83% were under fifty acres.[13] However, as the case studies above show, there was a considerable variation in wealth and methods of farming. In the 1950s, the Drennan farm at Carse Hall supported a farming family and seven workers, six of whom had been born on the farm. On wealthy farms such as this we can expect to find evidence of risky experimentation and large expensive machinery, such as portable threshing complexes. As we have seen, the Drennans owned five portable threshing mills, which they hired out to neighbouring farmers.

On smaller, but still commercial farms, such as the Murphys' or Wilsons', it is common to find a reliance on standardised foundry-made equipment, which was the product of international farming technology (Fig. 19). The Murphys, for example, owned a two-horse reaper, using a scythe to 'open' a grain field at harvest time. Both implements were used in the grain harvest in Ireland during the second half of the nineteenth century, but they were relatively late introductions to Mourne. The late Joey Murphy published an account of the stir caused in the late nineteenth century, when a returned migrant worker demonstrated how a scythe was used. He had learnt to mow while working as a harvester in Scotland.

> Having family ties in the Mayobridge district he was invited by a relative to mow a small field of oats in the townland of Ballydelaney. News of his coming spread like wildfire, and according to all accounts a 'terrible' crowd came to see him using the scythe.[14]

Fig. 19 Joey Murphy reaping oats at Hilltown, September 1941 (L1728/10)

On the smallest farms, such as Joe Kane's holding in Drumkeeran, almost all farm work was done by hand. Here we expect to find a reliance on manual labour, a high level of skill, and locally adapted techniques. Joe's expertise in spadework allowed him to utilise a ridge-making system of great refinement, where the size and shape of ridges were varied according to soil, slope, aspect, season, crops grown, and their place in a rotation.[15] At harvest, hay and grain were mown using scythes, but Joe also had experience in reaping oats using a hook. He estimated that he could reap, or 'shear', fifteen stooks of oats in eight hours, each stook containing twelve sheaves, and each sheaf made up of three handfuls of grain. Cereals were reaped when they were grown on narrow spade ridges, or when rain and wind had flattened the crop. One man working on his own could both reap and bind the crop, but Joe said that it was common when he was working on a farm where there was 'a spare woman' that she would be given the task of binding sheaves. Oats grown on the Kanes' farm were threshed using a flail, and the grain was winnowed in the open air, poured from a dish on to a sheet when the weather was dry and breezy so that the light shells of the grain heads were blown away. Hay was mown in June. Mowing with scythes was men's work but later stages of haymaking, such as shaking mown hay by hand, 'a wild sore job', were often done by women and children.

It is probably best to see the technological developments in farming during the past three hundred years as adding to the existing range of possible techniques rather than replacing them. As archaeologists have shown, it is still possible to find farming methods in Ireland, such as the ridge-making just mentioned, that were familiar to our prehistoric forebears. Farming methods were adopted that were most suited to a situation. Bob Lee of Cloverhill, County Cavan demonstrated this, using the example of harvesting grain. There was a mowing machine on the Lees' farm for well over a hundred years, but Bob was also skilled at reaping with a sickle. 'I can safely say … that I've helped to cut the harvest in Ireland in every way that it was cut, from the hook to the combine.' As on the Kanes' farm, sickles were used to reap oats that had become flattened or lodged by bad weather, but on the Lees' farm an undamaged, standing crop was cut using a horse-drawn reaping machine. Methods were selected that were most suitable in a particular situation, and it was not important whether they were very ancient or very modern (Fig. 20).

The case studies illustrate the fact that crops and livestock produced on farms remained fairly constant during the early twentieth century, although the scale and intensity with which they were farmed varied a lot. All of the farms included in this book were 'mixed', growing cereals and hay, potatoes, and often during the Second World War, flax. Horses, cattle, sheep, pigs and poultry were found on almost all farms.

Also constant were the basic elements of farming production: family farms. These have operated in one form or another for thousands of years, surviving invasions, wars, famines, political upheaval and revolutionary changes in the system of land ownership. The relationship between a nuclear or extended family and an area of land has proved one of the most enduring economic units throughout Europe and Asia for as long as records have

Fig. 20 In Irish farming, hardship has often led to ingenuity. This photograph shows Robert John Abernethy of Dunbeg, Ballynahinch, County Down, ploughing with a horse and a bullock in 1933. Ploughing with oxen had almost disappeared from Ireland by the early twentieth century, but farmers sometimes used a cow or bullock if a second horse was not available

existed. Economic theorists, notably Karl Marx, have been predicting the disappearance of smallholding families for well over a century, and they do seem to be under increasing threat. However, as units of production they have proved so resilient in the past that it is premature to write them off confidently. They provide the constant structures in which the lives recorded in this book were played out.

The above accounts show the complexities of managing even a single holding. Each farmer had to decide which crops and livestock to produce, and identify the most appropriate techniques in doing so. Most importantly, each farm required labour inputs from a range of people, whose efforts had to be co-ordinated on a daily and seasonal basis. The following chapters will show some of the ways in which this complex management of people was achieved.

4. Family farms

Despite an ongoing process of consolidation, farms in Ulster remained generally smaller than farms in Scotland or England, or in the provinces of Leinster and Munster. Near the end of the period covered by this book, in 1957, 79% of farms in Northern Ireland were under 50 acres and 59% were less than 30 acres. Only 5.6% of farms were over 100 acres. Many farmers used the system of short-term hiring of land, known as conacre, to increase their productive acreage, often by up to 25%. However, by the 1960s there was widespread concern that many farms were too small to be commercially viable. In 1963, it was claimed that between 50% and 60% of farms in Northern Ireland 'do not yield a level of income which can be regarded as reasonable in the light of present day circumstances'.[1]

Given their small size, it is not surprising that most farms relied largely on family labour. In 1938, a Ministry of Agriculture report estimated that three-quarters of all farm work in Northern Ireland was carried out by members of the farming family.[2] Oral testimonies are consistent in their view that the independence of a family from the need for outside help was seen as an ideal (Fig. 21). The family operated as a unit, and the interests of individuals were expected to take second place to securing the good of the whole. The grown-up children of the Murphy family from Hilltown and the O'Neills of Dungiven, for example, felt an obligation to help with harvest work on the farm even after they had left home, and arranged their holidays accordingly.

People are emphatic that at busy times, or where there was a shortage due to sickness or lack of children, any member of the family might be asked to do any necessary task. This meant that even young children were required to do work normally expected of adults. Joe Kane of Drumkeeran, County Fermanagh, was reared by his grandparents until their deaths; he was then sent at the age of seven to live with his uncle. Joe remained on this holding for the rest of his active life, inheriting it in 1953 when his uncle died at over ninety years of age. The two men lived on the farm by themselves, and so had to perform many tasks that would usually have been carried out by farm women. Joe learnt to make bread on an open fire when he was nine years old. His uncle could make bread, but not very well, and Joe particularly objected to the tobacco from his uncle's pipe, which often fell into the bread mixture! Joe went and watched a neighbouring girl making bread, and copied her method with surprising success. He was known for his cooking skills for the rest of his life.

Fig. 21 Three Wilson children with a turf barrow at Townavanney, County Fermanagh (L2727/3)

The need for Joe to take on adult work roles was obviously accentuated by the lack of other adults on his uncle's farm, but on small farms in general children were expected to behave like adults at as early an age as possible (Fig. 22). Children themselves often shared this aim. Rosemary Harris affectionately described the behaviour of small boys out with their fathers at 'Ballybay' fair in County Tyrone the 1950s:

> It was essentially a man's world … Perhaps it would be more accurate to say that it was a man and boy's world, for many of the farmers kept their sons away from school to help them in the Fair, and they came in, small imitations of their fathers, with sticks in their hands and serious expressions, their minds on cattle and not on larking about.[3]

Harris emphasises that on small farms in particular, childhood was not seen as radically separated from adulthood:

> All farmers, whatever their faith, wanted children because their help was usually essential to the economic running of the farm … Children on all farms began to help from the time they were about six. On the smaller farms particularly children rarely 'went to play' with any except their own brothers and sisters … boys passed into their teens still anxious to learn more of adult farming techniques from their fathers … A man's relations with his sons tended … to become progressively more difficult once they reached their late teens

… the father was free to select the succeeding son …

It was not the custom for even the more sophisticated farmers to give a regular wage, however tiny, to a son who remained on the farm; it was precisely because the son 'saved a man's wage' that he was wanted at home.[4]

Within the range of skills seen as men's responsibility, working with horses was the most highly valued, as late as 1950. Young men were encouraged to master the most difficult tasks, such as ploughing. Joe O'Neill of Dungiven, County Derry, began to learn to work with horses when he was about eight years of age:

> When I came home from school, my older brother [might be ploughing and] … he'd let me hold the plough. The Ransome's [wheel plough] was easy enough held, you know, and [it was also easy to] make the horses go out square, so that they wouldn't get over the chains … [I learnt] bit by bit … until finally he'd be away somewhere to look at something else, and I'd plough maybe four or five furrows … He showed me how to make the horses pull the plough … The horses less or more knew anyway.

Joe was also taught aspects of ploughing by a neighbour:

> I don't know whether I'm a very good ploughman or not, but I got a very good schoolin'. We had a neighbour, Micky Fearron [one of the local blacksmith's family] … it was him that showed me how to make a back and how to make a hint … He'd see me and he'd come over to me from [his own] … farm.

Fig. 22 Poling oats with a hay fork to make the crop easier for the scythesman to cut. This photograph was taken near Slieve Gullion, County Armagh in the 1930s (photograph Caoimhin Ó Danachair (L2121/3))

Bob Lee, of Cloverhill, County Cavan, began to learn to plough at the age of thirteen. He said that the caustic comments of neighbours watching from the side of a field were a great incentive to become skilled at the work:

> In them days, a man going past … would stop and look to see what kind of ploughing [had been done. If he thought it was poor, a typical comment would be] … 'What kind of hokin' match did he make here?' And if you did make a hokin' match, you'd hear about it! And that would be some morning maybe at the church gate, when there'd be a dozen people about or something like that! And you wouldn't like that now!

There was a wheel plough on the farm for as long as Bob Lee could remember, but he also enjoyed the more difficult and skilful task of using a swing plough. Many older Ulster farmers testify to the pride that went with carrying out a task as neatly as possible.

Women did horse work if required. This seems to have happened most often in families where there were no sons. Dolly and Isabel Lyons, for example, were two out of four sisters on their farm at Gannoway, County Down. They worked with horses almost every day, and carried out almost every task, apart from ploughing. Neither Dolly nor Isabel remembered having been taught the skills required. 'You were just brought up with them' (Fig. 23). This

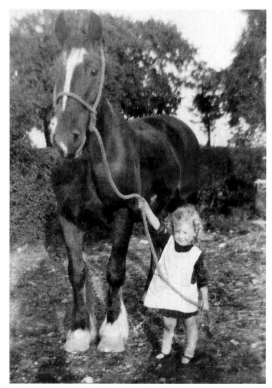

Fig. 23 Dolly Lyons, aged two, holding a Clydesdale horse at
Gannoway, County Down, in 1932 (L2726/1)

relaxed attitude also applied to other skills. Both women knew they could milk cows before they started school, but neither could remember actually learning how to do it!

Changes to techniques and the organisation of work on the farm were sometimes introduced due to the persuasive powers of the younger generation. Bob Lee's father usually kept two horses and a pony, and liked to breed foals from them, but Bob and his older brother thought that this created unnecessary difficulties:

> We used to have a great deal of trouble in the summer with a mare in foal, when it came to cutting hay or something like that … [We'd often] have to … leave the foal in the house. And [the mare] … would be a bit of a nuisance during the day, and the foal would be getting no chuck, and it would be in bad shape at home too.

The two boys eventually persuaded their father that it was unnecessary to keep all of the horses, and they arranged to borrow a horse from a neighbour, lending machinery in return.

Technical innovation could also be the result of conscious experimentation. Bob Lee described how he persuaded his brother to change his method of sowing grain on the farm. This provides a neat case study in technical innovation, and also shows the close relationship between the brothers, and their co-operative relationship with the demesne of the 'Big House' at Cloverhill:

> In my young days my father done all the sowing – wouldn't let anybody else sow – he done it out of a bucket with his hand … The eldest brother was very good at it too … [In later years when] I wasn't working at home, unless the brother … was stuck for a bit of help, and I'd go over … He came over to me one day and asked me, 'Would there be any chance of you coming over in the morning, and following the horses for me? I want to sow the orchard' – a hill that was just above an orchard that we had … I said, 'Alright' … [although] I didn't just like the idea [but] … I wouldn't say no to him, because him and I were great friends … I went up to the demesne and I saw the foreman [a local man], and I said, 'Would there be any chance of borrowing the [seed] fiddle off you, for sowing the oats?' 'Aw,' he said, 'No problem at all. Did ever you use it?' … So I arrived the next morning, and there was just a kind of long face enough! This wouldn't be the greatest job, especially when I knew nothing about it. So, I had got a wee bit of a lowdown from the foreman … and [I] kept [my brother] … carrying to me, and oh, in about an hour and a half, or an hour and three-quarters I had the field sowed, and that was the last time that ever there was anything sowed by hand. It was the fiddle after that.

On a farm with a well-grown, large family, a number of tasks were allocated by gender. In general, men were responsible for the heavy or skilled work associated with the cultivation of field crops (Fig. 24), and the care of large livestock. Women often looked after smaller and younger animals and assisted in field work, especially at busy times such as harvest. In the early twentieth century, however, their main responsibility was the processing of farm produce, for example butter- and bread-making, and the curing of bacon and ham.

The degree to which gender labour divisions applied, and the attitudes that sometimes

Fig. 24 John Adams with a horse-drawn potato digger at Lisbane, County Down in 1944 (photograph courtesy of Mr John Cooke (L2771/1))

accompanied them, are well illustrated by the following account by Mrs Mary Wilson, of Townavanney, County Fermanagh. On the Wilsons' farm, men were expected to carry out most work in the fields, and care of livestock including horses, cattle, pigs and sheep. The task of turf-cutting, Mrs Wilson said, was also 'definitely' men's work. Women were responsible for almost all housework, and the processing of food. The care of poultry was regarded so much as women's work that Mrs Wilson was amused at the idea of men taking it on. 'You daren't ask a man to help you! [with poultry] … They had no time for the like of that! … They just considered it women's work … they thought it was too easy and light for them.'

This was also the case in County Tyrone in the 1950s, when it was seen as an insult for a man to be asked to look after poultry:

> Looking after poultry and turkeys was women's work essentially, and neither the farmer nor his labourers would have dreamt of giving a hand in it. Once [the farmer's wife] … did ask … the hired man to help her and he was furiously indignant – locally any male over about thirteen or fourteen would have considered himself insulted by such a request.

(One exception to this seems to have been related to the greater commercial importance of deep litter poultry keeping.)[5]

Mrs Mary Wilson said that she did limited work with crops. She did not help with planting or gathering potatoes, but did work at stooking sheaves of grain, and raking and lapping hay. The expectation that women would help in the fields when it was necessary meant that housework had to be done ahead of schedule just before harvest. Even then, Mrs Wilson said, it suffered to some extent, some tasks such as washing clothes being left until the busiest period was over. On the other hand, her husband regularly helped her with making butter, which was usually churned on Monday mornings:

> My husband and I didn't approve of Sunday work – well, we did what was necessary. We used to keep the Saturday night's milk and skim it and churn it … [The cream] was put into the small churn and my husband usually helped me to churn it.

The following account of women's work is based on the testimony of three women from near Comber, County Down. Mrs Lily Cooke and Mrs Grace Montgomery are sisters, who grew up on their family farm in the townland of Lisbane. They, and a third sister, the late Mrs Teenie Magowan, helped their father John Adams with many of the tasks usually carried out by sons in a farming family. Mrs Ellen Gibson (née McClenaghan) carried out a wide variety of tasks on her family's farm in the townland of Drumreagh, but her account also describes the tasks particularly associated with women.

On the Adams's farm, the main crops were potatoes, grain, hay (including grass grown for seed), and turnips. Flax was also grown until after the Second World War. Because there were no sons on the farm, women's labour was vital in all stages of crop production. Spreading manure along the bottom of potato drills, a task known as 'scaling', was done by women, and women also helped with setting potatoes in drills before they were covered by a man using a drill plough. Women weeded growing potatoes, thinned turnips, and assisted with harvesting these and other farm crops (Fig. 25). The following is an account of the tasks involved in harvesting flax:

> [Rush] straps were made [to tie up] the flax. The rushes were cut … about a fortnight beforehand. The men cut the rushes and brought them home and stooked them up for a wee while. And then on a wet day they would have started and made the bands … and then they tied them in bundles … there was thirty-six put in each bundle … You had to count them when you came home from school and put them in bundles … When the people came to pull the flax, you gave them a bundle of bands, and that [did] three stooks – three twelves [i.e. three stooks of twelve sheaves or 'beets' each]. [They got half a crown for every stook they pulled.] … It was hard work … [and the farmers] had to keep their eye on them, for maybe they would have made wee beets … You'd know nearly by the look of them.

After pulling, the flax was placed in a dam to ret. The beets were placed 'slanty ways' and stones were then set on top to weigh them down. As a girl, Mrs Ellen Gibson helped with this work, which meant that she had to get into the dam. Women doing this work did not wear stockings, but went in barelegged, and sometimes barefoot. Others wore a pair of old slippers, or 'gutties'. After retting, the flax was removed from the dam for spreading. This was considered men's work:

They pulled it out of the hole with a clap … [that's] a long shaft with three [hooked] prongs on it … [The flax] was piled up along the lint hole, and they drew it out on a truckle car with no wings on it … That let the water run off it … Then the spreaders came, and they had to wear a rubber bag, and a string around the neck to keep them clean … My sister spread … They tried to spread it on [a] … neighbour's field, [where] the grass wasn't too long … they had to get it lifted … [before] the grass … [grew] up through it … Then it was tied [in sheaves] and put in a rickle … A rickle was just built like a wee house … [It sat] in the field … maybe a fortnight or three weeks. Then it was brought in and put in a [round] stack. And it was kept there, [and brought] … to the [scutch] mill about November times … It was scutched and then it was took to Ballynahinch … [where it was sold to one of] three mills round here at that time.

The women also helped in the hay harvest, forking the drying hay or 'lapping' it in wet weather. In the grain harvest they bound sheaves and stooked them (Fig. 26). Here too, the Adams girls were given tasks more usually done by men on farms. Grace Adams, in particular, helped her father with tasks such as making hay and corn stacks (Fig. 27), and both Grace and Lily worked with horses, helping their father, who was an expert horseman and won several cups at local ploughing matches:

We used the Tumblin' Paddy in the fields. Sometimes Grace drove the horses, and I [Lily] tumbled the Paddy … Sometimes sowing grain, I used to harrow it in. [We] never tackled ploughing … Sometimes we bedded and put [the horses] … in. If father was away at meetings at night, we had to give them water and give them hay. There were no boys in the family … and I had to do some of the jobs.

Women often had clearly defined tasks in the care of cattle. The Adams family kept about twelve cattle, both dairy and beef. Cattle were bought from dealers who visited the farm, rather than at fairs. Four of the cows were regularly milked, and this task was delegated to the girls as soon as they left school, at about fourteen years of age (Fig. 28). Lily Cooke estimated that it would take about ten minutes to milk a quiet cow:

Milking would have taken about an hour in the morning and an hour at night. Sometimes we … worked together, but if Grace was in the field working, I did it myself at night. The cows were brought in from the field about five or six in the evening and eight o'clock in the morning, after breakfast.

The girls not only drove the cattle to and from the fields, but sometimes also cleaned out the byre. They were also responsible for making butter. The farm's milk was processed at home rather than being sent to a creamery. A cream separator was used to remove the cream, leaving 'skim' milk, which was given to the calves. About twenty pounds of butter might be made on the farm each week. Some was sold to neighbours, and John Adams also brought the butter by horse and cart to a grocery shop in Ardmillan. Lily and Grace said that they stopped making butter at home after their mother's death.

Fig. 25 Lily Adams straightening up tossed oats at Lisbane, County Down
(photograph courtesy of Mr John Cooke (L2771/9))

Fig. 26 John Adams and his daughter Grace stooking corn at Lisbane in 1942
(photograph courtesy of Mr John Cooke (L2770/9))

Fig. 27 Grace Adams helping her father to load sheaves on to a cart at Lisbane, County Down, in 1937
(photograph courtesy of Mr John Cooke)

Mrs Ellen Gibson's family, the McClenaghans, had a byre that held twelve dairy cows, and she said that her mother brought butter made on the farm to a weekly market in Oxford Street, Belfast, by horse and cart, and in later years by bus. Her mother also sold eggs in the market, from a small stall. As elsewhere in Ulster, the care of poultry was the special responsibility of women. Mrs Gibson gave an account of how women managed poultry flocks on farms in the area. This shows her detailed knowledge of rearing and feeding poultry, but also provides an example of women operating a network of mutual help with one another, independent of the farms' men.

There were about fifty poultry on Mrs Gibson's home farm. They were of various breeds, including Leghorns, Wyandottes, Anconas and Rhode Island Reds.

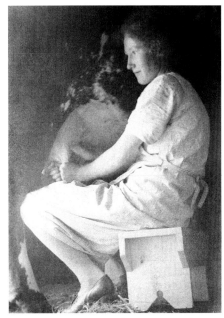

Fig. 28 Grace Adams milking a cow at Lisbane (photograph courtesy of Mr John Cooke (L2771/7))

> There was no foxes then and the hens wasn't closed in at night … If you saw a neighbour's hens out early in the morning, well [you knew] them was good hens, they were good gatherers – good laying hens. And you went along to see if the neighbour would gather you two settings of eggs [for hatching] … and you would ask if she wanted them swapped, or did she want money for them … [In return for swapped eggs] you had to take your eggs [for eating], and you had to give her a day or two to pick them, because you didn't want a great big egg, … because sometimes they would have died in the shell when they were coming out … Sometimes in a big egg there was two eggs in one – a double yoked egg.

Very small eggs were also rejected, and also eggs with thin shells, as a hen might put her feet through these while she was sitting on them.

> There was no incubators then, and you had to bring them out with clocking hens… If there was two clockin' hens … you would have set the two hens, and then whatever birds came out you put them to one hen. And the corn was took to the mill then, and you got oatmeal made, and you would have fed the wee birds on the oaten meal – brought them up. Then when the corn was cut, if it was a stubble field, and there was much corn left on the field, you would have got a house, a wee house took out to the field, and the birds [were put in that] … They didn't get meat then, they got nothing only water [all the] time they were in that stubble field. And you kept them there as long as you could till the bad weather come, and then they were brought home. The corn would have been cut maybe say, the end of August, and maybe they got staying September, and maybe October … That was just bringing them up to laying and then they were brought home … Roosters

were killed [at about 8 weeks] for a pot of soup … There was no broilers or anything … [After being brought home the hens were fed]. There was no hen meal or anything then. There was just maybe yellow meal steeped the night before. And then you just took the bucket out and couped it on a flat stone or something, and … the hens ate away at that.

Until the late 1950s, most eggs produced on the McClenaghans' farm were sold to traders from the town of Lisburn. The traders provided crates and these were collected every week. This egg trade stopped because it became unprofitable, as meal had become very expensive.

The McClenaghans also kept turkeys:

> Whatever farmer's wife had a turkey rooster, you had to take your [turkey] hen there … When she was sitting, you got her below your arm and you took her … across the fields – [it could be] a brave wee distance. You had to mark her in case she got mixed up, for maybe the woman had a dozen [turkey] hens. And you let her stay a day or two. Then you had to go back for her and bring her home, and if she didn't lay inside a fortnight, you had to take her back again … You set, maybe, eight below a hen, and maybe if the turkey stopped laying and took a rest, and she started to sit again, you took her back and got a second laying … If she clocked, you put the wee turkeys till her – for she was able to look after them.
>
> You had to gather nettles and dandelions, and boil eggs, and this is what they were fed on. There was no chick mash then … You had to watch them in case they got a shower, for if they got wet they were sure to take bad or something. Then, when it came on Christmas, you had to feed them up well … you would have put the meat in a dish and set it on top of a bucket so that they could stand and eat – they didn't like to stoop down. And [you] kept them eating to fatten them up for Christmas … You had to make sure you put them in before dark, because if they got up into the bushes, you couldn't get them down! Though there was no foxes, if they got wet they were sure to take something.

At Christmas, dealers called to the farm, and the women sold the turkeys to the highest bidder. The farm men brought the turkeys to town by horse and cart, but the women got the money made from their sale. 'They did all the work!'

The McClenaghan family usually kept four sows on the farm, of several breeds, including Landrace, York and Large White Ulster:

> I fed the oul' sows – they were just rough fed … [A local man,] Robert Jordan, [and my father] killed them … We had to boil the water for them coming … in the boiler outside … You had to have the water plumping when they came … They hit them over the head with a mallet to start with … Then they scraped them in the boiling water, and hung them up. Then they slit them down and took the heart and liver out of them … We kept the heart and liver a very odd time, [but] they [usually] went with the pigs … You had to have your name down [with a dealer] … to take [the pigs], and they went off the next morning … They went somewhere in Belfast.

When pigs were killed for home use it was often found that the whole pig carcass was too much for one family, and Mrs Gibson said that it was common for a neighbour to buy half of it. The remaining half provided the farm family with bacon, ham and ribs throughout a winter.

Some of the most important changes in family work on farms during the early twentieth century were related to women's work. The overwhelming impression of all accounts of farm work in the early twentieth century is of a range and depth of skills that allowed adult family members to work together in a tight division of labour, as in the description of pig-killing just given, and also to fill the place, at least partly, of anyone who, perhaps through sickness or emigration, was not available for work on the farm. However, the modernising movements of centralisation and standardisation had profound effects. These sometimes involved the learning of new skills, but also meant that many old skills began to become redundant. This was particularly the case with the food-processing skills associated with women. Butter-making, bread-making and the curing of meat all moved out of the farm and into specialised dairies, bakeries and meat-producing plants. Changes in the scale of farming changed women's roles also. Commercial farming of poultry and pigs became especially large-scale and intensive, and milking machines heralded the end of hand-milking in the intimacy of a small byre.

This deskilling of farm women was noted all over Europe from the late nineteenth century onwards. A description of the situation in Germany in the 1930s could well be applied to most parts of rural Ireland:

> The role of farm women became increasingly less satisfactory as the nineteenth and twentieth centuries progressed. Her age-old role as food and clothing processor dwindled in importance as participation in the market increased. However, this original role was replaced by increasing her share of farmyard work: feeding pigs and calves, milking cows … etc. Her jobs appeared to become 'dirtier' and more toilsome as traditional roles declined … As a result, the stereotype of the farm woman with the 'black apron and Wellington boots' has become more powerful.[6]

Throughout the period covered in this book, a very similar process was well under way in Ulster. Rosemary Harris believed that in County Tyrone in the 1950s, 'the pressure to do yard work was greatest on the wives of poorer farmers in general and hill farmers in particular. The more "mountainy" the farm and the poorer a man's equipment, the more time he had to spend in his fields and the more essential it was for his womenfolk to do the yard work.'[7] The loss of skills, and the possibility that women who stayed on the farm would become simply unskilled and low-status labourers, may help to explain why, throughout Ireland, many more women have left rural life than men.

5. The neighbours

We have seen that in general, farming people aimed to make their family as economically independent as possible. On small or medium-sized farms, where a family had an able-bodied man and woman at its head and at least one grown son, little help was needed from outsiders. However, even in these situations some help was needed at busy times of the year or if an emergency arose, such as family illness. At these times, people tended to look to their neighbours for help. Families where there were very young children, or none, or where emigration or death had reduced the family labour supply, needed to call on outside help more frequently. In these situations, or where the family did not have enough resources to provide all of the equipment or horse power needed, economic links with neighbours were of necessity much closer, and longer term.

A network of ties of mutual help covered the countryside, and the relationships involved were known by special terms. Fig. 29 shows the distribution of the most common terms found in Ulster. These could apply to working arrangements, either between individual

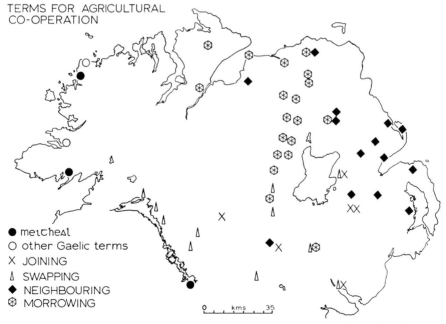

Fig. 29 Terms for co-operation in Ulster, based on a questionnaire sent out by the Ulster Folk and Transport Museum in 1977

Fig. 30 Lint pulling on the McSparran's farm at Cloney, County Antrim (L2703/9)

Workers

1. Pat 'Wee' O'Hara worked for the McSparrans in the family shop in Glasgow, until the middle of the First World War, when he returned to the Cushendun area to avoid conscription. He worked periodically on the McSparran farm for many years afterwards.
2. Willie 'Dan Roe' McNeill was a local, landless labourer.
3. Pat O'Neill was hired on the farm in the 1920s, and when he was much older, as a temporary worker.
4. Jim O'Neill was the longest serving labourer on the McSparran's farm.
5. Dan 'Ganty' McKay was from a small farm in Layde, but laboured for the McSparrans.
6. Charlie Martin was a temporary labourer.
7. John O'Hara, the nephew of Pat O'Hara, also worked as a temporary worker on the farm.
8. Dan McNeill lived in a cottier house in Glendun and worked as a farm labourer.
9. John McKay of Ranaghan was a farm servant.

Farmers

10. Pat 'Susan' McCormick had a farm in Glendun.
11. John 'Susan' McCormick had a farm in Glendun.
12. Charlie Douglas, a second cousin of Archie McSparran, had a farm in Layde.
13. Alex Douglas, a second cousin of Archie McSparran, had a farm in Layde.
14. Gus McKay had a farm in Knocknacarry.
15. Neill O'Neill's farm was in Fallinerlea, beside Drumnacur.
16. Alex O'Hara went to Australia in his youth, but at the time the photograph was taken, he was farming in Knocknacarry.
17. Dan McCormick was a farmer's son, who later had his own farm in Ardicoan.
18. Jimmy McKay had a farm in Layde.
19. Joe Magee farmed in Unchina townland in Glendun.
20. John 'Dan Roe' McNeill had a small farm in Glendun.
21. John 'Archie' McNeill had a farm in Glendun.
22. Henry McKay had a farm in Ranaghan.
23. Paddy MacDonnell had a farm in Cloughglass.
24. Jack McKay had a small farm in Layde.
25. Dan McKeegan had a small farm in Glenaan.
26. Patsy McAuley had a farm in Sevagh.
27. Frank O'Boyle was married to a first cousin of Malachy McSparran's father. He had been a merchant seaman whose wife had a farm in Glenariffe. He travelled about 8 miles to the lint pulling, further than anyone else.

Others

28. Mary Murray worked for Malachy's mother. Mrs McSparran always had a woman to help her.
29. Malachy McSparran was only about three years old when the photograph was taken, and since his five sisters were all born after him, Mrs McSparran had no female help at home.

farmers (*comhar*, neighbouring, swapping, morrowing, etc.) or the working groups formed for bigger, short-term tasks (*meitheal*, gathering, boon, fiddler, camp, etc.).[1] However, it is important not to attempt to classify these relationships too rigidly. Farmers responded to situations as they arose, and – as with farming techniques – a wide range of possible arrangements could be put in place, depending on the need and the individual relationships of people involved. During the twentieth century there was an ongoing increase in government regulations and documentation related to running a farm. However, as in the previous three centuries, government officials in particular were repeatedly frustrated in attempts to impose codified regulations on farming people. The flexibility of working arrangements is a clear example of this. If the need arose, farmers could call on help from relatives, neighbours, and paid help, all at the same time.

The complexity of possible arrangements is well illustrated by an example from Hornhead in County Donegal. These involved two families, the Durneens and the McHughs, who lived about a mile apart. Mick McHugh explained that the working relationship began with an arrangement to lend and borrow horses to make up a two-horse plough team. 'They ploughed with our mare and then we ploughed with their mare. That's how they got in contact and then they hired me for six months.' Mick explained that 'There was a crowd of us in the house, and there was no call for me, and the [the Durneens] … asked my father'. Mrs Durneen hired Mick first; when she died, he was hired by her daughter, Mrs McFadden. He stayed in the house with the McFaddens and was hired by them for thirteen years, doing all sorts of farm work. When Mrs McFadden's brother, William Durneen, bought a farm on Hornhead in 1939, he contracted Mick's brother John to plough land and to cart stones for him, John earning thirty pounds for the work. Mick said that the family did not have a 'swapping' relationship with the Durneens, but 'they would help you and you would go help them'.

The different types of people that might be called on for help with short-term tasks are also well illustrated by an instance from the Glens of Antrim. The McSparran family of Cloney engaged in relations of mutual help with neighbours, known in the Cushendun area as 'morrowing'. However, large groups of helpers, known as 'boons', were sometimes required. As on many Ulster farms early in the twentieth century, the hiring of a portable threshing machine each year necessitated large-scale co-operation. Another such occasion was the flax or 'lint' harvest. A photograph taken at a flax-pulling on the McSparran farm at Cloney, County Antrim (Fig. 30) shows something of the range of relationships used to assemble such a group. The people shown in the photograph were a mixture of family members, full-time farm workers, temporary hired helpers, and neighbours. Malachy McSparran's father returned neighbours' help in flax-pulling not by going to work on their farms on the 'day for a day basis' commonly reported, but by giving the services of his bull to anyone who helped. The McSparrans summed up this arrangement up by saying, 'It's the bull that pulls the lint.'

Within all this complexity, however, we can make some generalisations.

Partnerships between individual farmers

Working arrangements between two neighbouring families could last for many years. Almost anything could be swapped or borrowed: equipment, seed, livestock, land, or labour. On tiny farms in the Rosses in west Donegal, for example, basic foodstuffs might be exchanged. On the Wards' farm in the townland of Keadew, near Burtonport, milk and butter were important elements in the family diet. Each person was given a cup of milk at dinner, and men coming in to the house from work in the fields could help themselves to a cupful from a container kept on the dresser. At night the 'skim' of the milk from the container was put into a crock. Once a week all of the skimmed milk collected was made into butter by the farm women. Hugh Ward could not remember any butter or milk being sold, but milk was commonly given to needy neighbours. 'If my neighbour had no milk … and I had milk, I kept them going on milk until such time as their cow calved. And all the neighbours about would take milk to them if they had some.' More negatively, in this world of hardship, an essential element of the household economy on many small farms elsewhere – the pig – was not kept. Hugh Ward said that the only part of the Rosses where pigs were kept was Lochanure. The reason he gave for the reluctance of people around Keadew to keep pigs was that the obligation to share with neighbours made it uneconomic. 'The trouble was, if you slaughtered a pig here in them days you had to divide it out with your neighbours.'

This shows that, while the exchange of help could be generous, it was not unlimited. Some measures of exchange were adopted. For example, many farmers would labour for one another on the basis of a day for a day. The practice of lending and borrowing horses to make up a two-horse team was also common. In these instances, farmers had a clear view of what constituted a fair exchange. A 'morrowing' relationship near Cookstown, County Tyrone, ended abruptly when one of the participants took revenge for what he saw as the misuse of a horse he had lent his erstwhile partner.

The incident began when the farmer, Mr Dan McKay, was ploughing land. He had only one horse and this meant that the ground had to be ploughed twice to achieve the required depth. He had just begun the work when a neighbour approached, and offered to lend him a second horse. This was agreed, but Mr McKay realised that the neighbour would want something in return. As he expected, after his own ploughing was finished, the neighbour asked if he could borrow Mr McKay's horse:

> He wanted mine and I couldn't say no. And he kept mine … at night. I says, 'Well, I have this mare fed bravely … and … I don't want you … to give her first grass hay' – that's hay with the seed slapped off it … 'as you know yourself it's no good for an animal that's fit to work'. [He asked for more nutritious upland hay, and some oats – 'corn' – to be given instead.]
> So he had my mare working for two or three days anyway … and I thought he should have been bringing her home again … So I went down … It was after dinner hour, and I skited into the stable, and the stand that mine was in was crushed full of first grass hay, and the other one was clean with some of the [good] upland hay, where his horse was standing.

I wasn't in too good temper … There were a … servant girl, and this … girl [said] … 'Your mare's working bravely this weather'.

Says I, 'I suppose'.

'Aye,' says she, 'she was out here before seven o'clock these mornings. And more than that, them hen houses there … it was your mare that pulled them out … to the fields.'

His own brothers had big horses, and this man that helped him had big enough horses available, but they took it out of mine. So I wasn't in feeling in too nice temper.

'Aw,' he says, 'I'm glad you come. You'll need the mare home … I didn't know whether to send the girl up with her or not.'

'Ah,' says I, 'I think if you had just brought her out to the roadside there … and turned the rope, she would have come home [on her own]' …

Says he, 'I'd like to get the corn in'.

Says I, 'That's what I want to see. Well, I'll either sow it or harrow it … Will I bring the corn out and sow it, or what?'

'Aw,' he says, 'Mary Ellen will carry it to me.'

He didn't want me to sow the corn, you see. He thought I mightn't sow it right …

Says he, 'You can take the horses'.

Says I, 'I suppose I could'.

So I got the horses in anyway, and got tea, and a good feed of corn for the mare … She had more corn than she could bear …

[When it came to setting up the harrows] the swingle trees was lying on the fair … If he had been a decent man I would have turned it over and let mine get the short one, you see, and done the heavier bit. But says I, 'We'll just let him get a swing of his own' … So mine was a big number anyway, and his was a wee boy, a tight wee thing … and I … gave them a wean of belts along the side … . So when he was done sowing, I had the harrowing finished … The sweat was running out of … [his horse], and let him stay all night to soak in it! And I got the mare up the road … and … gave more to eat and let her go to bed. So that finished the morrowing with him.

One of the many interesting things about this account is that the servant girl, an onlooker, also decided that the neighbour had abused the relationship.

Differences in wealth had some influence on the types of exchange between farmers. As we have seen, the McSparrans of Cloney exchanged the services of their bull for labour. Sometimes differences seem to have arisen which meant that a farmer felt that he could no longer exchange help with a neighbour. Rosemary Harris has recorded an example of this from the Ballygawley area of County Tyrone in the 1950s. This involved two brothers-in-law, 'Fred' and 'Paul', who had co-operated for some time. Paul started to work more with a cousin, 'Bill', and Fred withdrew from the relationship:

Although Fred gave as his reason for his withdrawal the fact that the group had become unwieldy there was probably another reason, for his departure coincided with Paul's buying a tractor. Once he had done this Fred could no longer work with him on the basis of equality. In fact Paul had always been the slightly more influential partner, since he contributed not only his own labour but that of … [his paid labourer] as well. Moreover, his farm was bigger than Fred's, so that not surprisingly more work was always done at Paul's than at Fred's. Once Paul had bought the tractor his position vis-à-vis Fred was bound to become overwhelming. Paul's cousin Bill could still make a valuable

Fig. 31 Flax pulling at Keenan's farm in Leitrim townland, near Hilltown, County Down, around 1935. The people shown are, from left to right: Mick Keenan, Matthew Fearon, Dolly Murray, Brendan Hudson, Daniel Keenan, Hugh Murray and Patrick Rooney (photograph courtesy of Mrs Mary Savage L3447/3)

Fig. 32 Flax pulling at Keenan's Farm in Leitrim townland, County Down, around 1935. The people shown are, from left to right (beside and on cart): John Murray, Matthew Fearon, Patrick Rooney, Hugh Murray, Dolly Murray. (Front) Brendan Hudson, Patrick Keenan and dog, and Daniel Keenan. The horse's name was Paddy, and the dog's Carlow (photograph courtesy of Mrs Mary Savage L3447/2)

contribution because [he had a] … background of agricultural contracting [and] … was a skilled tractor operator and something of a mechanic. [Paul was not] … Bill's skills therefore made a contribution almost as valuable as Paul's capital.[2]

The limited extent to which some farmers could direct neighbours who came to help them is suggested by an incident described by Dan McKay:

> One day the neighbours come to me, and I had potatoes [to dig and gather] … I had given the neighbours a whole lot of plants, cabbage plants, and one day didn't four of them come with spades to dig for me. And I had to gather for them all! [Mr McKay had difficulty gathering potatoes because of a weak hip] … They come to dig and I couldn't very well say 'Come you boy, and gather!'. They were doing me the favour and I had to do the best I could to keep it moving. There be's some good neighbours to morrow with … and some would want to use you.

The threat of scarcity and the uncertainties of farm work, especially in the changeable Irish climate, could lead to tension, especially if both farmers in a working relationship needed the same task completed quickly. Most people are emphatic that these potential sources of conflict were dealt with by intelligent negotiation, but many knew of relationships that had ended in bitterness. Hugh Ward of Keadew recounted a particularly dramatic incident from County Donegal. Hugh said that this had occurred on nearby Cruit island:

> There was three men on Cruit island, and they used to help each other out in the springtime … cutting the seaweed … So this day the three of them was out, and they were coming in with a cargo of wrack, and the little boat they'd with them went on a rock … Well this lad went in to shove her off the rock. He went out on the rock – the tide was coming in, you see. And he shoved her off – he was hanging on to the side of her, you see. And one of the boys in the boat … thought the boat was going to capsize, and he got hold of one of the pins … for putting the oar in, and he started hitting him on the knuckles … you know, telling him to let go of the grip. He says, 'Never again would I go out with them boys'. So that finished the partnership.

In this part of Donegal, local tensions often came to a head at the summer fair held in the town of Dungloe on 4 June each year. 'There was a great go for fighting at the summer's fair … If some two had a grievance, they were sure to meet that day in Dungloe and settle it.' Such conflicts, however, were not allowed to become so widespread that they interfered with friendly working relationships between neighbours in general. Their help was too greatly needed. This became particularly the case when male members of a family left home as seasonal migrant labourers, a very common practice in the Rosses. Women left on the farm then had to cope with routine farm work as well as their normal household duties. For some heavy tasks, such as mowing hay or grain, the help of male neighbours was seen as essential.

Despite the possibilities of conflict, relationships of mutual help were often very warm and co-operative. Neighbours were often careful to ensure that they gave a fair return for any help. This is clearly illustrated by an example from the Ederney area of County Fermanagh, where help between individual neighbours was known as 'swapping'. Joe Kane and his uncle, of Drumkeeran, County Fermanagh, often had no horse on their tiny holding, so they sometimes needed help from neighbours who owned a horse. The horse was required for tasks such as drawing home turf, taking manure to fields, bringing home hay, and – especially in the period of increased tillage during the Second World War – ploughing and harrowing. If help with the last two tasks was available it could ease the strain on the resources of a small farm considerably. The cost of paying for extra seed and fertiliser during the war represented a worrying risk:

> The big man could get over the loss better than the poor man … [This was why] the like of me there that would have no horse … I'd go to my neighbour, maybe say Jim Moohan and … he'd come a day … and I'd give him two days of a swap.

The horse could be hired, but Joe Kane said that most men preferred to have work done on their farm rather than be paid money. The arrangement of two days' manual labour in return for one day's use of a horse was to some extent flexible:

> You have to go by the weather too. You could go to the man to give him a day, and it might rain most of the day. Well then, you'd have to give him another day, or if you were a bit awkward, you just let him do with that. There's some men used to do that, but the way I used to do, I gave the man a decent day … maybe half a day it might rain … [so] the next day you'd give him another half day forenenst it. You see, we worked through other here, one way and another. People gets on, you know.

In some cases, help given might be remembered and the obligation to return it fulfilled years later. Cormac McFadden, who was raised on a very small farm in the Roshin hills in north Donegal, remembered being sent as a boy to help on a neighbour's farm, in return for help given to his father when the McFadden children were too small to work either on their own farm or the neighbour's.

Teams of workers

The range of tasks for which teams of workers were recruited was as wide as that for which partnerships between individuals were used (Figs 31 and 32). In arable farming, help might be required for all stages of crop production: the preparation of land, sowing and planting, care of growing crops, harvesting, and processing and storing.[3] In the period between 1930 and 1960, the occasion when help was most needed was when a portable threshing machine was hired to process the farm's grain crop (Fig. 33). The arrangements made when large-scale threshing was planned involved both men and women.

Fig. 33 Threshing mill in operation, powered by a Ferguson tractor (L2090/9)

Mrs Mary Wilson of Townavanney, County Fermanagh gave a clear description of the organisation required. The work required the help of up to fifteen men. A steam threshing machine, drawn by horses, was pulled from farm to farm. The machine used in Townavanney was hired out by a creamery in the nearby town of Kesh, and neighbours would agree among themselves the order in which it should travel around the farms in the district. The arrangement had to be adjusted from time to time, especially if the weather became wet, but Mrs Wilson gave a detailed account of how the work was organised on the day the thresher arrived on her family's farm:

> There would be three or four carts carting in the corn, and there would be a man … cutting the straps … off the sheaves, and there would be a man placing it into the thresher, and there would be someone then watching the bags [of newly threshed] corn … so that they didn't overflow. And then … the straw that came out after being threshed … was built into big stacks for the winter and was used [as fodder] for the cattle.

Women were kept equally busy, in the house. Preparations for the threshing day could begin up to two days beforehand, with the baking of bread, and killing, plucking and cleaning of about six hens:

> [I had] to have help in too indeed … I usually had a girl working and … she scolded away and cooked away … It was the done thing that you would have chicken, for the men at the thresher always liked their dinner … at about half twelve … They would be very hungry, and you would have chickens and carrots and peas and beans and potatoes … and then rice afterwards … and then a cup of tea.

The pattern was similar in many parts of the country. A description of threshing arrangements on the Adams's farm near Comber, County Down, confirms this. John Adams hired a thresher twice a year, in November, and again in January or February. The machine – which belonged to a local quarry owner – stayed on the farm for a day, or a day and a half. The Adams women did not help with the threshing, but prepared food for the fifteen or sixteen neighbours who might come to help. 'They got their potatoes and meat … You had to have the meat ready the night before and the vegetables all prepared.'

At these very busy periods, women were expected to rearrange their ordinary routine so that extra work could be fitted in. During harvest, for example (Fig. 34):

> Mother would have stayed at home in the morning and made the dinner … and then she might have come out and stayed till tea time, and then went home and made the tea. [The tea and food were] all put in a big basket and all carried out … [Things like washing clothes] had to be done later … or the cows had to be left [until] … later too, if you were busy outside in the field … We always tidied up the house – brushed [it] – [but] we had to work hard while the weather was good … If a shower came, you got to do some wee job.

Fig. 34 Tea in the harvest field at Lisbane, County Down, 1942. Lily and Grace Adams with John Adams and Willie McKee (centre) (photograph courtesy of Mr John Cooke (L2771/6))

Work teams of all sorts were known to be occasions for practical jokes, and friendly rivalry between workers. For Joe Kane, occasional travel to a more distant farm made the day's work an adventure:

> There was a clergyman in Ederney one time and he was away down home near Garrison, [about twenty miles from Drumkeeran] and the brother and sister wasn't in good health … and he asked a few of us would we go down … setting [potatoes] … So he gathered four of us up and he sent the housekeeper down till cook for us … His sister wasn't in good health, and the brother was far back with the crop – I think it was around the twelfth of May … We … set a good lot for him … He just only asked … a few people to go down for a day … You didn't like to refuse him, when he asked you. Oh, it was a day's outing for us too.

Neighbours around Drumkeeran also sometimes worked from farm to farm when hay was being moved from fields into a shed or haggard. Up to twelve neighbours would help. Four men might be positioned in the meadow forking hay on to four carts. Four men operated these while another four were in the farmyard, either building stacks or putting the hay into a shed. Joe Kane emphasised the enjoyable aspects of working together:

> Ach, it was a kind of pastime, you know … There used to be a big day putting in the haystacks – they'd have bottles of whiskey, do you know … they were the greatest haystacks ever made! … You had no bother getting help if you produced the bottle of whiskey.

Differences of status between people who helped might be reflected in slightly different treatment, however:

> Well then … the older type of men [and men who provided horses and carts], they were taken away to the [good] room for their dinner, and there was a fowl killed and the bottle of whiskey was up there … it was a kind of an honour … The servant men and the working men [went into the kitchen] … and sometimes … if the man was any way generous, he might give bottles of stout to the ones in the kitchen and sometimes they didn't get any drink at all … There wasn't much counted on the working man that time, you know.

The overwhelming emphasis in people's testimonies is of the warmth and co-operative spirit involved in mutual help involving both pairs, and larger teams, of neighbours. Bob Lee of Cloverhill, County Cavan summed this up very well. He remembered as many as fourteen people helping the Lee family to harvest their oats. The Lees in turn would go to work on other farms when requested. Mr Lee was emphatic that ties of mutual help between neighbours around Cloverhill were characterised by an eagerness to help, even when men were looking to one another for help to perform the same sort of task at the same time:

> You'd be reckoned as a very awkward man, if a neighbour [asked for help, and you] didn't fall in line with whatever [he wanted] – if you wanted to cut oats today or dig potatoes, and [the other man] … also wanted to dig, well, you'd hang back – one or the other. 'Well maybe it'll suit better to do it your way' … I never knew any nastiness … in my lifetime.

In this part of Cavan fields were generally small enough that two neighbours working together could often harvest one another's crops in the same day, even if this meant working until eight or nine o'clock at night. Rather than hanging back from helping one another, Bob Lee said that neighbours working in groups often competed in a friendly fashion to be the fastest worker.

He gave an example where six spadesmen were working together in a field:

> They wouldn't be there too very long … till you would be trying to see if you could pass me. Quietly, you know – and maybe you'd be a better man at the spade than me, you see. Or you might be better than him. And, whoever would get out first with their ridge or whatever they were doing, then they were reckoned to be the best. But there'd be somebody else who would be bound to try before night to see would he pass him by.

In Mr Lee's account, as in many others, women's main role was to provide tea, bread, butter and jam to the workers in the field. The socialising that accompanied breaks during communal work and the celebrations that followed its completion were an important factor in making it enjoyable. A *meitheal* called for pulling flax was especially festive:

The way they'd gather the meitheal was with a quarter barrel of Guinness, or maybe two quarter barrels. And it would end up with a whole spree that night! … I never pulled flax, but I used to hear them [talking] in the local [pub].'

In the world of small farms around Drumkeeran in north-west Fermanagh, the connection between working together and the *céilí*, or 'cayleying', was still strong until the 1950s.

Neighbours around Drumkeeran who worked together also socialised together. In his youth, Joe Kane 'cayleyed' two or three nights each week:

I used to *céilí* in Willie Jones's. Willie lived over in Gortgeran but he left at the time of the War … they were all great musicians … There used to be great nights in it, there'd be fiddling and dancing. Then the 'upper house' they called it, that was his uncle and aunt. They lived farther up the lane, they were great musicians too, and there used to be a lock of neighbours round … there used to be maybe nearly a dozen, and they'd get up and [set] dance to the music … There were other houses we used to *céilí* in too … They'd be playing cards … they might be playing for something – they could put up a rooster or something like that … and there'd be tea, and there'd be a jolly night.

Joe had occasional visitors on his own house at night, but rarely more than two or three. Casual visiting between neighbours did not always involve intensive socialising. Rosemary Harris observed that in County Tyrone in the 1950s, 'in the [small farming] hill district if a man was used to visiting another's house it caused no comment for him to enter and sit down for an almost silent evening.'[4] Whatever form it took, however, most people agree that socialising connected to neighbourly co-operation has declined. Joe Kane attributed the decline in the *céilí* to two main causes: emigration and television.

The decline of mutual help, and its associated socialising, is a common theme in many testimonies. Hugh Ward of Keadew, County Donegal, said that in the early decades of the twentieth century, groups of neighbours frequently came together to work on a farm. In his local area, such a group was known as a 'gathering' or a 'fiddler'. He gave the following example to show just how large such a group could be in the past, but also how the practice declined in more recent times:

Why they called it a 'fiddler', there'd be a dance that night, maybe in some country house – the house they had gathered in to dig the ground for. Or … if there was an empty house about somewhere, they got the lend of it for the night. And there'd be a lad would come and play the fiddle. And they would dance away there till twelve o'clock … I mind my oldest brother … called a fiddler … I think it was after Saint Patrick's day … There was a lot of digging to be done … and he got thirty-six spades digging … but in the later years, I mind a lad up the road … took badly, and we said we would gather, you know, and dig the ground for him … but there were only four or five of us came. And that finished it … That would be now, about the outbreak of [the Second World] War.

When Hugh was a young man, more than a dozen people would regularly gather on winter nights in one another's houses around Keadew to talk, tell jokes and drink tea. This was known as 'caleyin' or 'granyin', words that are anglicisations of the Irish words *céilí* and *greannmhar*. Like Joe Kane, Hugh believed that modern inventions, such as television, were responsible for the decline in caleyin.

The degree to which informal working relationships really were characterised by generosity and willingness to help, and the degree to which they have disappeared, have been the subject of debate by academics. It has been suggested that people describing these relationships can be expected to describe the past in normative terms, that is, in terms of what should have been the case. It has also been pointed out that the testimonies of older people, that informal socialising has declined, may be little more than a description of their own experience. In modern western society, older people do face problems of increasing isolation.[5] However, contemporary commentators were also clear that increasing mechanisation was affecting the extent to which people co-operated. By the 1940s one agricultural investigator, John Mogey, found that in the Hilltown area of County Down, one-third of all farms depended on hiring a tractor or a horse team to fulfil their wartime quota of ploughing. He commented, 'This is a measure of the degree to which the older partnership principle has been superseded, and also of the effects on agriculture of the pre-war depression years'.[6]

It was not always the case that mechanisation led to a decline in mutual help. As we have seen in the case of portable threshing machines, technological developments could actually increase the requirement for short-term help. However, overall, technology has lessened the need for physical labour in farming, and this, combined with the ongoing decline in labour-intensive arable farming, can be seen to have lessened the need for frequent mutual exchange.

The connection between working together and socialising, and the effects of technology on this, were well summarised by John Mogey in 1947:

> Everywhere [in Northern Ireland] there are memories of the local ceilidhe houses, but in almost all areas families have become isolated one from another. The base of the older social life, the system of mutual aid between neighbours, has now ceased to be essential with the introduction of improved implements and greater wealth. In our opinion, once the necessity to work together has disappeared or is disappearing, the customs of the age also vanish. There is therefore no point in pleading for a revival of the friendliness of the countryside in the old forms. Friendliness and good relations between neighbours still exist. The aim for the future must be to build upon what is good in rural society and to erect a social framework suited to the modern needs.[7]

The decline in help is always described with regret. Whatever tensions may have arisen, in general people emphasise the celebratory aspect of working with neighbours. Farming families may have co-operated initially because they had to, but once begun, the relationships involved often proved warm and enriching. Mrs Mary Wilson's description of the feelings associated with threshing probably reflects emotions generated on many other occasions also. For Mrs Wilson, these threshing days were very happy, because they were complementary to harvest thanksgiving services held around the same time in local churches:

> It was a time of really thanksgiving … everyone helped each other and they were all very, very kind and good … and even they would stay, you know, on after dark at night, to help finish up … In fact, it was the top item of the year … that you had the corn safely gathered.

6. Hired help

One big difference between urban and rural life in Ulster during the early twentieth century was that working for a cash wage was relatively rare in the countryside. This was the result of a long-term trend all over Ireland, which had gone on almost uninterrupted since the years of the Great Famine in the 1840s. Emigration, and a change from arable to pastoral farming, led to a great decrease in the number of farm labourers.[1] This was particularly true in Ulster, where, as we have seen, farms were run largely by family labour. The decline continued throughout the first half of the twentieth century. In 1940, there were 19,800 paid male full-time farm workers in Northern Ireland. By 1960, this had dropped to 8,200.[2]

During the Second World War, the decrease in agricultural workers was temporarily reversed. Increased production, and shortages of labour in general, led the government in Northern Ireland to introduce tight controls on the employment of people identified as agricultural workers. National Service Officers could refuse to release an unemployed agricultural worker for any other kind of work, and could require agricultural workers engaged in other work to return to agriculture.[3] Short-term employment of workers became extremely important in Northern Ireland during the Second World War. The need for this was well summarised by the Ministry of Agriculture:

> As mechanisation becomes more and more highly developed, the more do the needs for labour become seasonal. Give a farmer a tractor and all the necessary equipment and he can place a very extensive acreage in crop with very little labour, but when harvest comes round and this crop has to be taken out, the amount of labour required for a few short weeks is almost unlimited.[4]

Schemes were introduced to recruit large numbers of temporary workers through Labour Exchanges, including those in Belfast, for harvest work. In 1944, 130,000 people were recruited to work under the Harvest Labour Scheme.[5]

The strategies adopted by families to supplement their labour resources in peacetime varied depending on the availability of family labour and the scale of particular farming operations. On the O'Neills' farm outside Dungiven, County Derry for example, requirements for paid labourers were infrequent and short-term. There were nine children in the family, five boys and four girls. This ensured a labour supply that was sufficient for most routine work on the farm. In later years, when some members of the family had gone to England to work, they came home to help at harvesting. However, for major harvest tasks, help from neighbours and some paid labour were also required. Extra help at the potato harvest was easiest to arrange, because children of between eight and fourteen years of age could be hired to gather the crop. It was much more difficult to find the extra hired adult labour required for the flax and grain harvests. Joe O'Neill said that 'At that time of year, a lot of the working class people … they'd be away to England working … There'd be a surplus [of labour] in the winter time … but they wouldn't be here when you really needed them.'

The family attempted to offset their labour requirements by harvesting the flax crop in stages. One year during the Second World War, when a particularly large amount of flax was grown, the crop was sown on three different dates, the earliest being at the end of March. All of the flax grown on the farm was steeped in one dam, so harvesting in stages made processing easier. It also spread labour requirements, so that less was required at any time. The first three acres harvested were pulled by the family, and the next by a team of four men employed for the task. These men then went to another farm for a short period, before coming back to the O'Neills to pull the remaining flax. The O'Neill family members were able to manage the tasks of carting flax to the dam and steeping it themselves. Local schoolchildren were easily found to help with removing the retted crop from the dam, and spreading it to dry.

The family employed three or four temporary workers for tying oats, when these were reaped using horses. Joe O'Neill said that two men could easily tie an acre of oats in a day. A portable threshing machine was hired each year for about a week from a local family, the McCartneys. The O'Neills had an arrangement with two neighbouring farmers for help in making up one another's threshing teams. It was particularly easy for the O'Neills to make up their share of the team, as they almost always had two or three workers available from within the family. The two neighbours would have to make subsidiary arrangements with others to make up their part of the team.

The pattern of employment on most Ulster farms shows the same flexibility as many other aspects of the small farm economy, where adjustments often had to be made very quickly. Mrs Mary Wilson sometimes employed local girls to help with housework on the family farm at Townavanney, County Fermanagh, especially at busy times such as threshing, when, as we have seen, a local girl would be brought in to help prepare the meal for men working at the threshing machine. Mrs Wilson had a series of weekly paid girls, some of whom lived on the farm for short periods, who would undertake some farm work as well as housework. Her husband employed men to work on the farm. Some Donegal men were hired as harvest workers, and would stay on the farm for a few weeks in autumn each year. Another local man, from Boa island, worked on the farm for around five years as a weekly paid labourer.

Hired servants

The flexibility of arrangements between farmers and their paid workers seems to have arisen partly from the possible range of personal relationships involved, as well as the needs of the farm. Personal relationships were particularly important in the situations of close proximity in which hired farm servants and their employers often lived and worked.

The hiring of farm servants was well established in Ireland by the late eighteenth century, but their recruitment at hiring fairs seems to have reached a peak in Ulster in the late nineteenth century, when these were held in around eighty towns throughout the province. The system began to go into steep decline after the First World War and the introduction of unemployment schemes, particularly that put in place in Northern Ireland in 1937.[6] By this time, government officials recorded that the hiring fairs that survived, such as the one held at Limavady, were largely seen as holidays and that very little actual recruitment of servants took place.[7] The last Ulster hiring fair was probably held at Ballycastle, County Antrim in 1947. The disappearance of the fairs, however, did not mean the complete end of the hiring system. As late as the 1970s it was occasionally possible to find farms where elderly people, who had been hired as servants many years before, had been given the right to stay on the farm during their old age.

There was a lot of variation in hiring arrangements. The most common pattern was that servants were employed at fairs held around the twelfth of May and November, and then went to live on their employer's farm. Their lodging was counted as part payment for their labour. The main monetary payment was given as a lump sum at the end of their six-month term of employment. However, almost any element in this arrangement could be changed by negotiation. Some hired people lived at home, some were paid weekly, and in many instances arrangements were agreed outside the hiring fair. Notwithstanding the difficulties in defining the hiring system, it is perhaps the area of working life in the past that most intrigues people who remember it.

Hired servants were usually young. Until 1923 and 1926, when a minimum school leaving age of fourteen was introduced in Northern Ireland and the Irish Free State respectively,[8] servants might be hired for full-time work when they were as young as seven years of age. Hiring usually represented a first stage in people's working lives and, especially in County Donegal, usually lasted until they were old enough to take over their own family's farm, become a seasonal migrant worker – often to Scotland – or emigrate permanently. People who hired servants usually did so to fill gaps in the family labour supply on small farms.

Bríd Coll, of *Doirí Beaga* in north-west Donegal, was employed as a servant by a local family for three years, beginning in 1932, when she was eight years of age:

> If there was a lot of people in one house, maybe these [other] people had no children to herd their cows for them, so come March, they went to look for somebody to mind the cattle – *buachaill bó* – well, I wasn't a *buachaill* [a boy], but … that's how I got the job. You went, say, around the beginning of April and you stayed in that house until the end of October and you got whatever shillings … and you came home … There was three women in the house [where I worked] and two men always, and then the other two came from Scotland … I went to school every day when I was there … then … down to *Machaire Gathlán* [to work].

The small size of many farms meant that servants and the farming family often had to live together very closely. This could lead to situations of great conflict, described in some oral testimonies as slavery, and the oral and written records of hiring contain many allegations of brutal treatment, including physical beatings, neglect, sexual abuse, and, in a very few instances, even murder. However, it is also important to emphasise that intensely warm relationships might also develop, where hired people appreciated being treated 'as one of the family'. Bríd Coll's comment on the family that employed her was clear. 'Oh by gosh, they were good to me.' The kindness of some employers is also well illustrated by Mrs Mary Wilson's account of how a young local man came to work on the farm at Townavanney, County Fermanagh, in the 1930s (Fig. 35):

> His mother and he lived in a cottage a short distance along the road and my husband always thought him a rather nice lad. So [his] ... mother took ill and she only remained for a few days until she passed away, and after the funeral was over he was all on his own in the cottage, and Thomas thought him very lonely. Like, he was only about seventeen at the time, so he brought him over to [live in the Wilson's] ... house, and he stayed there for a number of years and worked for them ... There was only Thomas and his mother and father there at the time ... He was a good lad, very, very good ... he worked with the horses and milked and did all the farmwork ... My husband always said that he tried to make him save all the money he could, for he talked about going to another country, and ... he said he was very saving and very wise, and didn't waste his money ... He left here and he went to Belfast, and he didn't like it. And he came back – he had a sister ... and he came back to her and he just stayed around. He died early in life ... He was very, very good to my husband's mother ... He treated her as if she was his own mother.

The career of James Ennis

The following account of hiring is based on James Ennis's testimony. James was unusual in that he was hired from a children's home, and since he had no family farm to go back to, he remained a hired man for many years. His career as a farm servant stretches well into the period after 1930.

James was born in Dublin in 1910; both of his parents died while he was too young to remember, and he and his two brothers were sent to Nazareth Lodge children's home in Derry city.[9] James was reared in the home until he was fourteen years old, at which age his guardians began to try to find him work. The two types of work most preferred, according to James, were the army and farm service:

> They had to keep them till they got a job, and it was mostly always farmers that they were put in till, because the like of us had to go to a place that you could be put up at night, you see ... You couldn't start roaming the streets, you know. So they had to try and get you a place like that, or some of them went into the army ... That was convenient too, because the army kept them.

Fig. 35 Thomas Wilson and a young hired man at Townavanney, County Fermanagh (L2727/2)

James's older brother, who had already left the home to work on a farm near Dungiven, County Derry, heard of a possible place for James on another farm. The farmer came to Derry and was interviewed by staff at Nazareth Lodge, who then decided that the work he was offering was suitable. James was sent to the farm, as a servant. The farmer, from the townland of Templemoyle, had one son of about twenty-five years of age, who worked on the farm with him. The labour of these two men was sufficient to run their small farm of about 50 acres, so James was employed mainly in helping the woman of the house, who had a form of dermatitis which meant that she found difficulty in working with water.

James was taught to milk the farm's three cows, and two or three goats, and also to care for the pigs and poultry, collecting and washing eggs. After this was finished he was expected to help with work in the fields. The farm's crops were mixed: oats, potatoes and hay. Although two horses were kept, most of the crop cultivation was carried out by manual labour. The oats and hay were cut with scythes, and the potatoes harvested using spades rather than a mechanical potato digger. James was given a bed in the barn attached to one end of the house. There was no other furniture, but James found it 'nice and clean.' He ate with the family, sharing their food:

> There was no other place for it. Just the table and four chairs … and an oul' open hearth. Breakfast consisted of a bowl of porridge, a cup of tea, and a soda scone. [Dinners were] rough … just passable, but there was usually some meat.

When he was asked if he socialised with the family after work, James laughed:

> What are you talking about? Sure you worked till dark. You worked till bedtime … You just come in and got your supper and went out again and started the same as at eight o'clock in the morning!

He was given time off on Sunday mornings to go to church. This had been one of the requirements made of the farmer by the staff of Nazareth Lodge. James said, however, that other requirements were not so well attended to:

> The bargain was that they were to supply me with my food, and keep, and clothes you see … [but] they didn't buy you hardly anything … maybe got you something second-hand in Dungiven … They never bought you anything new, you know.

James did not know if he was supposed to be given wages. He received none, except that on his last day at the farm, the farmer's wife gave him a half-crown. James said he left the farm because he was not very happy there. A neighbouring farmer, George Kane, offered him work, and he accepted, although it was not the end of a hiring term. The Kanes' farm, like the one he had just left, was a small holding relying on mixed production. There was, however, a little more mechanisation: for example, a reaping machine was borrowed during the grain harvest. It was the prospect of doing a man's work that, for James, was one of the main attractions of his new situation:

> I just started off with horses whenever I went to this other man. I was only fifteen then, you know. Round about that anyway … I learnt everything from him, aye, ploughing and carting. I'd rather have had that as the other job … I'd rather be out in the fields. I was more or less doing a woman's work you know, cleaning eggs, and washing dishes, and one dang thing and another.

Another attraction of Kanes' farm was that it was good fun. George Kane, although in his forties, was subject to his widowed mother, who owned the farm. 'She was the boss.'

James was delighted with George's wayward behaviour. The first incident that he recounted concerned the half-crown that the woman on his first employer's farm had given him:

> [George] came up for me, d'you see, to show me the ropes and all. And coming down the road, he says … 'Hey, did the oul' doll give you anything?' I says, 'Aye, she gave me half-a-crown.' 'You wouldn't lend it to me?' he says … anyway, I lent him the half-crown and I never seen it again!

James also described some of George's techniques of obtaining drinking money, one of which was to conceal extra bags of crops in the cart he was taking to Dungiven market. It then fell to James to look after the drunken George, and prevent a row developing at home. Escapades like these, James said, enlivened the three years he stayed working on the Kanes' farm:

> He was the best of crack … He was good value. I liked the value. I was a young chap, and there was always plenty come in at nights … They used to call it … [the] *céilí*, you know. Some nights the house used to be full. Who could tell the biggest lie, you know   Rough farmers just come in for a bit of a yarn, you know, and we'd have went to some other house the next night.

The preference among hired farm servants for smaller farms, because these were generally 'friendlier', has been widely recorded. In James Ennis's case, his lack of a family home seems to have made this even more important:

> I'd nowhere else to go. I was a stranger there, you see. That was my first time out – I'd never seen a being till I come out there … Where was I going to run?

James said that the Kanes had hired him because they found it cheaper to keep him, and pay him a small monetary wage at the end of each six-month term, than to pay a farm labourer who did not live on the farm, and whose weekly wages were largely paid in money:

I'd three pound with him the first six months. And sure, three pound, how far would that go, paying a man by the day or the week? … It's economics is the whole thing. Simple as that. He allowed he might get me cheaper than he'd bring in a man.

After three years James's pay had not changed, so he decided to move on. In May 1928 he went to the hiring fair in the town of Limavady but, although he waited all day, he did not find work. The next day he went to Derry city, where one of the largest hiring fairs in Ulster was held in the central square, the Diamond:

> You always stood at the Diamond. You had to have a wee parcel, you know, below your arm, and then they knew you were looking for a job. If you were well dressed or anything … they didn't interfere. They'd look at you, a pair of oul' trousers with about ten holes in them, and … an oul' parcel … Even if you'd nothing in the parcel, as long as you had [it] … they knew you were looking for a job. Sort of code, you know.

James had no home to go to if he was not hired, so the fair was a particularly worrying time:

> You were worried stiff … Because you'd nowhere to go that night, unless somebody took you in, you know. Oh, you had to hire somewhere. You were tied, you see. There was no other jobs available at that time.

Many people remember hiring fair days for drinking, dancing, and fighting. James's memories were not so colourful:

> Sure it took you nearly all day to get hired, for heaven's sake. You were running about here, and running about there … You've no idea what it was getting hired. You daren't have moved from the Diamond for fear you'd miss, you know, a job. You had to stand there all day.

James was eventually approached by a farmer. This man asked what sort of work he could do, and what previous experience he had. He made a contract with the farmer for a six-month hiring term, payment being his keep, and £10 at the end of the term. This last part of the deal pleased him very much. He was taken aback, however, when the farmer said his farm was near Ballymoney, some forty miles away:

> I didn't even know there was such a place in the map. See, we were reared in the home there, we knew nothing about towns or nothing.

James said that farmers sometimes preferred to hire servants at a distance, since this meant that there was less chance of the servants leaving once they had arrived on the farm. The farmer gave James a half-crown as a token payment, known as an 'earls' or an 'earnest'. He told James where to catch a bus for Ballymoney, which he did next morning. His new master's son met him with a pony and trap.

When James moved to Ballymoney, in north-east Ulster, he also moved from working on small farms to farms that, by Northern Irish standards, were large. His new employer, James Getty, had a farm of about 200 acres. The land varied in quality, but James considered Getty to be 'a big, rich farmer'. Mr Getty's grown-up son worked on the farm and also another man, who was employed in six-month hiring terms but lived in his own home, which was near by. The size of Getty's farm, and the number of workers, was reflected in a clearer division of labour between them.

James Getty kept four, and sometimes five, horses. His son had the position of 'first horseman', which meant that he performed the skilled work of ploughing and making potato drills. James Ennis worked as 'second horseman,' which meant that he carried out 'all the carting and all the dirty jobs, you know. Drawing out manure to the fields – anything like that.' The locally hired man worked as a general farm labourer. Even on this larger farm, however, the division of labour became blurred, especially at busy times. Most of James's time was spent in general farm work. 'Tying corn, tying grass-seed, building corn-stacks. You know, the usual thing about a farm – snedding turnips and thinning turnips …'

James slept in 'a first class room' of his own upstairs in the farm house. The family and workers ate in separate rooms. James and the other hired man, and two maids, ate in the farm kitchen. One of the maids was local; the other was from County Donegal, and was also a hired servant.

James stayed on the Gettys' farm for six months. In November his contract was not renewed, the farmer saying that there was not enough work to justify keeping a hired man throughout the winter. A local woman, however, told James of a farm some forty-five miles away, near Mallusk in the south of County Antrim, where he might obtain work. She gave him an introductory note, and when he presented this at the Mallusk farm, he was employed on a hiring contract. The owners of the farm were two brothers named Barnes, who ran a solicitor's firm in Belfast. James and another hired man were responsible for carrying out all the work on the farm.

James was employed as a horseman, the other man being given special charge of cattle. The two men slept in a room in the farm yard, above the stables. This was sparsely furnished, with two beds, but it was 'nice and clean and all'. The workers, who sometimes included labourers employed on a daily basis, ate in the same room as their employers but at separate tables, except for the housekeeper, who ate with her employers. Relationships between James and his employers seem to have been relatively formal, but his monetary wage had again increased. He received £13 at the end of the six months for which he worked on the farm.

The following May, at the end of the hiring term, he went to Coleraine hiring fair. He travelled back to the north coast region because he had made friends there, with whom he could stay the night if necessary. He went to the Diamond square in Coleraine, where servants looking for work gathered, and did not have to wait long before being engaged.

The farmer, George Caldwell, had a farm near Portrush, only a few miles away. James was offered his keep, and again was to receive £13 at the end of the hiring term.

Caldwell's farm was large; as his children were young, he employed two hired men and one day labourer to work it. The other hired man had been working on the farm as first horseman before James was employed, so James was given the lower paid position of second horseman. He was pleased, however, with his sleeping quarters, a room of his own in the farm house. As in the Barnes's house, the family ate in the same room as the workers, but at a separate table. After one term, James moved on again, this time to a farm about one mile outside Ballymoney. He described his next employer, Dan Carson, as

> a fine man to work to … There were a boy put me on till him, he says he was looking for a man like. There was no hiring … on that day, but I went down. I'd an oul' bicycle you see … and I went down and seen him, and he says 'Aye, just come on ahead … Start the morrow morning.'

Carson's farm extended for more than 300 acres, but a lot of the land was peat bog, which he let to neighbouring farmers for cutting fuel. Mr Carson was newly married and, as well as employing James and another man as servants, had day labourers working on the farm. James was again given a bedroom of his own in the farm house; he and the other workers ate in the kitchen of another house adjacent to the main dwelling. James stayed on this farm for three and a half years, working mostly with horses. The task he found most exhausting, he said, was harrowing, since when one was ploughing the handles on the implement gave some support. He had little energy for socialising, especially at busy times in spring, but did occasionally go to dances in Ballymoney. He described an incident relating to one of these, which illustrates the number of hours a farm servant was expected to work:

> The boy that was hired along with me in that place … we were at a dance in the town hall … and I looked at the watch. Says I, 'Hey, we'd need to run. Four o'clock!' Says I, 'We'd need to run if we want to get an hour's sleep.' And out we goes, and we'd bicycles, you know. Ten minutes it took us out or less. We jumped on the two bikes and away like hell. And we met the farmer in the yard! 'Did you feed the horses yet?' – by the way he thought we were only rising! I was no' even in the yard hardly. 'Man, that's great!' he says 'Throw them horses a bite, ye boy ye!' … That was shortly after four o'clock in the morning. Man, I was raging, I didn't run far that night!

It was while working at Carson's farm that James met the woman he eventually married. She was a local woman, and they met when she came with other workers to help with harvesting the farm's potato crop.

After Carson's, James went to work on a neighbouring farm, where he was employed as a hired man for the last time. He lived on the farm for some time, but when he got married he rented a room for himself and his wife in the town of Ballymoney. The unemployment benefit scheme was instituted in 1937, shortly after he went to his last employer, and he claimed that this, more than anything, led to the end of hiring:

> Man, they did not like that, hey, putting on the stamp. They knew, you see, once that carry on came on, they'd get nobody to work to them … Before that stamp came out, people working to contractors on roads, or the public works as we called them, they had a card of their own, but a farm labourer couldn't get that card. No way could he get that card. Therefore, he couldn't leave the farmers, for he couldn't get a job nowhere. It was well tied up, mind you – crafty. They'd it tied up, you see, that we had no card at all … This card only came out when I was in [my last employer's farm] … in the thirties. And even if you weren't in a job, even if a contractor could of give you a job, he daren't – you're a farm labourer. So then the unions fought, and got this farm labourer's card out – a green card, the stamps were green … Then they done away with that card. Everybody just had the one card then. So that finished the farming. You just went and got a job anywhere, as long as you had the card stamped.

For some years after his time in farm service James did casual work, both locally and, on two consecutive summers, in south-west Scotland. In his early forties he found a job in a local bacon factory, and worked there until he retired. He ended his life in a house near the centre of Ballymoney.

Workers on the Drennan farm at Carse Hall, Ballykelly

Hired farm servants were not the only farm workers to live on their employers' farms. Workers might also be given a house or cottage for themselves and their family. By the early twentieth century, this arrangement seems to have been confined to a small number of very large farms, and its main interest is that it shows one end of a range of employment relationships.

The Drennan farm at Ballykelly, one of the richest in Ulster, was especially unusual in that workers not only lived on the farm, but were often actually born there. In the late nineteenth century there were ten labourers' cottages on the farm at Carse Hall. A farm labourers' wage book for 1924 lists nineteen workers.[10] John C. Drennan, who farmed Carse Hall between 1916 and 1958, said that during his youth there were between twelve and fourteen men permanently employed, but by 1958 there were seven, all of whom had life-long connections with the farm:

> When I gave up Carse Hall, all the employees had been born, with one exception, on the place – [they had] lived there all their lives. My Farm Manager came as a child to the place … and he was reared by an aunt of his that was on the place.

The farmworkers' cottages were provided rent-free and each had a small garden. In the 1950s, these gardens became infested with eel worm, but the householders were given a rood of potato ground each season, for which they provided their own seed.

Mrs Drennan employed two maids and 'a woman' in the house. The maids were unmarried and lived in the house, eating the same food as the Drennans. They had alternate Sundays off, and when they worked on Sunday, they had Saturday evening off. Maids would stay about five years, after which they got married, leaving for the wedding ceremony from the Hall.

Farm workers were given fixed working hours. When John Drennan took over the farm, the hours were from 7 a.m. until 6 p.m., but this was later changed to 8 a.m. until 5.30 p.m. Early in the twentieth century, John Drennan said that the average weekly wage paid to workers was one pound. The wages book from the farm lists payments in 1924, which range from 13s. 4d. to 22s. 11d. During harvest, a half-crown overtime pay was given, irrespective of the number of extra hours worked. Tea was also provided to the harvest workers in the afternoon.

The large labour force at Carse Hall allowed a degree of specialisation that was very unusual in Ulster. Apart from the farm manager (also known as the land steward), there was a shepherd, a byre man, and several men who worked with horses:

> At one time we had five skilled ploughmen … Latterly, even until I gave up, we had three men who could still plough with horses, but we did most of the work with tractors at that time, barring the ploughing – we nearly always did very deep ploughing for root crops with horses.

Two men had very special responsibilities. One attended the pumping station, which was necessary to carry excess water off the rich reclaimed arable land beside Lough Foyle, on which the farm of 640 acres was situated. This took up a lot of time during winter. The Drennans also employed a groom, who was responsible for the reputation of the farm's Clydesdale stud, the largest in Ireland (Fig. 36):

> [The] stud groom did nothing else … only look after the horses … to prepare them for … show … For instance, for Balmoral Show in the month of May, I would start with these horses in the month of September in the year before … You had to look after the hair on the legs, they had to be oiled … and their hooves kept in shape … They had to be shod, and reshod, and all sorts of things. It was really a full-time job.
>
> We had a lot of paddocks that we kept the show horses in, and we had a little house in each paddock, and [the horses] … had to be fed night and morning in those paddocks … But I was able to give him a lot of assistance … In fact many a night he and I slept together in a box with a mare waiting to foal. We just lay there on some straw and waited patiently.

The resident farmworkers had a large number of dependants and these people provided the Drennans with a short-term labour supply at busy times, particularly for planting potatoes or thinning turnips:

Fig. 36 Clydesdales at the Carse Hall Stud. The men holding the horses are, from left to right: William Montgomery (blacksmith), Hugh Montgomery, Bob Martin, William Loughrey, Samuel Martin (in charge of the stud), Samuel Irwin and Thomas Martin (photograph courtesy of Mr T. MacDonald and Mr D. Bigger)

> All the wives … and some of the youngsters … up to about ten or twelve years of age [did the thinning] … The wives all insisted on being allotted so many drills of turnips … and they were paid so much a hundred yards for thinning [them] … Some would take a dozen [drills], some as many as two dozen … I've seen as many as forty [women and children] … out in the turnip field … I never had to employ anybody [from outside Carse Hall] until the latter days.

Both Mr and Mrs Drennan stressed the happy working relations on the farm. 'It was like a family'. No one was ever sacked, even though the Drennans believed that the farm was heavily overstaffed, pointing out that in the late 1970s farming at Carse Hall was carried out by just two men. John Drennan said that, 'I just couldn't pick up enough courage to say, "Look, I don't require your labour any further" … they were all of them there all of their lives, so I decided I would get out myself instead!'[11]

Differences between employers and employees at Carse Hall were blurred, partly because Mr and Mrs Drennan regularly worked alongside their staff. Mrs Drennan ran the dairy, and John Drennan not only helped the stud groom and the shepherd, but also helped to look after the pumping station at nights, because the man employed to do the work was frightened to be left there alone. The lack of rigid division of labour was apparent during the annual stack building. This skilled work was carried out by the byre man, the land steward, the man in charge of the pumping station, and John Drennan himself.

Joe Kane's working life

During the early twentieth century, country people looking for work outside their home farm tended to move between short-term casual work and longer-term contracts, as opportunities arose. Until he was sixty-five, Joe Kane regularly supplemented the farm income from his small Fermanagh holding by working for other people. He found it easy to find temporary paid work around his home townland of Drumkeeran, at both harvest and turf-cutting. As in many parts of Ireland, a turf cutting team, or spade, was made up of three men. One man cut the turf, another filled the turf barrow, and a third wheeled it away from the turf bank for spreading. Joe said that filling the barrow was usually the hardest work. However, this was not always so. In some bogs cutting could be more difficult, while on very

Fig. 37 Joe Kane on his bicycle, beside Lough Erne, in the 1930s (L3175/5)

soft bogs wheeling the barrow could be most strenuous, as the wheel sank into the surface and the wet blocks of turf hung over the sides. A man hired to make up a 'spade' expected to be given the most difficult task.

The working arrangement could be made much happier if the person doing the hiring acted with consideration. One such man employed Joe for six days in the bog at three shillings a day, a rate of pay thought to be 'powerful' at the time. Although he had to work later in the day than usual to earn this money, the farmer who hired him lent him a bicycle on which to ride home in the evenings (Fig. 37). He was also given 'breakfast, dinner, and tea in the evenings'. After his own turf had been cut, the farmer arranged for his girlfriend's family to give Joe another five days' work.

Joe also worked for more extended periods with several local farmers, on what he described as a 'hired' basis. Unlike hired servants such as James Ennis, however, Joe did not live on his employer's farm, and did not have to wait until the end of the six-month 'term' for pay. He was paid weekly but was employed on a term's contract. He valued this, as it gave him the security of constant work. He was hired first with a local man, Jonnie McCourt, in 1931, at the age of eighteen:

> He asked me one time to go till him to work … and then when it came to the hiring time he asked me to hire. He [had] asked me to go on a day basis first … I suppose it was a kind of trial … [I had work on the farm] wet and dry … Some men wanted you on good days … but on a wet day they didn't want you, and you could have a whole lot of days [without work], unless there was some special work on. You might, with someone … get

half-a-crown a day in the bog off them. And that would be great, you know. But [I was sure of] … a shilling a day … with Jonnie.

The security of employment and the good food that the McCourts gave him during working hours were so valued by Joe that he worked on their farm for nine years. He started work around half-past seven in the morning, and stopped at eight o'clock in the evening. At harvest time, however, he might work until nine o'clock for no extra pay. During winter he was kept busy threshing corn, cleaning drains, cutting hedges, or digging ground, a task that was often commenced in January.

Joe continued to seek labouring jobs throughout his working life. His last job was with the Forestry Division of the Department of Agriculture of Northern Ireland; he remembered, with regret, planting conifers on ground that had been his neighbours' smallholdings in Drumkeeran.

Hugh Ward's career as a migrant labourer

Like the small farmers of north-west Fermanagh and other poorer parts of Ulster, many people in the Rosses region of west Donegal had to rely on activities other than working on the family holding to provide a living for their families. State institutions, with varying degrees of success, attempted to develop activities such as knitting, weaving and fishing, but the most important source of income, apart from farming, was migrant labour. Just before 1900, it was estimated that more than one third of the cash income of an average Rosses family came from migrant labour.[12] Hugh Ward of Keadew remembered whole families, including young children, closing up their houses and going away to work for the summer. Donegal workers most often went to hiring fairs further east in Ulster, or to Scotland, in squads, as potato harvesters known as 'tattie hokers' or 'tattie pickers'. One of Hugh Ward's brothers was a hired farm servant in the Laggan district of east Donegal, but Hugh's own experience was in fish curing and working in the Scottish grain harvest.

Up to one hundred workers went each year as fish curers to Scotland from the Keadew district. The great majority were women, but the fish curer by whom they were employed also tried to hire a 'crew' of three young men to work in the curing yard. The young men would be employed to roll barrels and build them up in tiers, work that was considered too heavy for most women. The men were paid more than women. When Hugh first went to work at curing in 1931, women were paid sixpence an hour, while men were paid eightpence an hour.

Hugh worked in the curing yard as a packer, and it was with the packer that the curer in Scotland made arrangements for work and travel. Hugh was responsible for assembling the squad and obtaining tickets, with money that the curer sent to him. Money was also given for meals eaten during the journey. The packer received three pounds in 'earls' money, which meant that he was legally bound to work for the curer for a whole season. While the workers were in Scotland, one pound a week was given for food.

Fig. 38 A herring station in Lerwick, in 1935 (photograph PO 25888, by kind permission of Shetland Museum)

Hugh Ward worked at fish curing in places as far apart as Lerwick in Shetland and Yarmouth in south-east England. Working arrangements seem to have been fairly similar in many ports. In Shetland the herring boats were unloaded by the fishermen into small 'bogies', which were then pushed up a rail track to a long wooden trough known as a 'farlan'. Women stood along the sides of the farlan gutting the fish, and then throwing them into tubs (Fig. 38). When these were full, three young men carried two tubs between them to a larger 'roosin' tub where salt was thrown over the herrings with a scoop. The fish were then removed from this and put into barrels in 'tiers'. A full barrel weighed more than three hundredweight.

When the barrels were packed, coopers would inspect them. A group of ten 'crews', or thirty people, would have two coopers working along with them. The herrings were graded into 'fulls', 'mattie fulls', 'matties' and 'small'. If a cooper decided that a barrel was not properly graded, or that too much salt had been added, he could empty the barrel back into the roosin' tub, so that it had to be packed over again.

The full barrels were left standing for a day, by which stage the herrings had settled down, so that several extra layers or 'tiers' had to be added to fill them. After this the coopers put lids on the barrels, and they were left for another nine days. More fish were then added, as well as 'pickle'. The cooper bored a hole in the side of each barrel and pickle was poured in through it. This completed the curing process.

The fish workers were housed in small wooden huts. Each crew of three workers was given a hut, and Hugh Ward remembered the line of huts stretching for several miles out of Lerwick towards Scotland Point. Socialising in the evenings was intense. Accordion players were very popular, and dancing could continue right through the night. Hugh believed that 'it was the sport that kept them going – the fun'.

Hugh went to work in the Scottish grain harvest one year, shortly after having spent a season in the fish-curing yard at Frazerburgh. He decided to try to find harvest work, and so went to a boarding house in Perth used by migrant labourers. There he met four older men from the Keadew, Arlans and Cruit districts of the Rosses who were looking for a worker to make up a harvest squad. Compared to the squads of tattie hokers, the grain harvesters formed an elite in the world of seasonal migrant labour. Hugh said that harvest teams often consisted of four workers reaping with hooks, and one person tying and stooking. Hugh was employed for the latter tasks. The squad was paid by the acre, and aimed to cut two and a half acres each day, i.e. half an acre for each worker.

In good weather, work would begin as early as eight o'clock in the morning, continuing until six or seven o'clock in the evening, with a short meal break around noon. The reapers cut the grain and twisted the bands with which the sheaves were tied. Reapers from Gweedore in west Donegal were famous for the speed at which they could cut grain. This was partly achieved by the reaping technique, which was seen as distinctive. Right-handed reapers held the grain to be cut with their left hand. Each handful was then let fall on to a heap held against the reaper's left leg. When a bundle large enough to make up a sheaf had been cut, the reaper pulled out some straws using the end of his hook, twisted them into a 'strap' for tying, and then set the sheaf on top of this. Hugh followed behind, tying up the sheaves and making them into stooks.

The men were given sleeping and cooking quarters, often in a vacant house, which was then known as 'the Irishman's bothy'. The person working at tying and stooking, in this case Hugh, was responsible for cooking food.

> I used to be in maybe half an hour before them … And there was a butcher used to come to the farm twice a week and I would get a shilling each from them before I'd go down, the day the butcher was coming … and you want to see the dish of meat I would get … it was all steak … Well, that would keep us going for a couple of days … Then he came another day a week. So you had, say four of the working days, you had steak.

Each member of the team was 'on the same divide' when money earned was apportioned. Hugh Ward said that the rate of pay in the year on which he worked in the grain harvest was three pounds per acre. This meant that if two and a half acres were cut in a day, each man would earn thirty shillings. This was considered very good earnings, as many workers at the same period were only earning thirty shillings a week.

After the mid-twentieth century, the number of Donegal people engaging in migrant labour declined sharply. Hugh Ward related this to a shift in working patterns begun by the Second World War.

> After the War broke out, there wasn't as many going from around here. But a lot of the men went to the public works – They were round recruiting here – some for agricultural work, some for public work … The result was that the younger crowd that used to go to the potatoes wasn't going at all – you know, twelve- or fourteen-year-olds … Well, times got better then in Scotland and England, and there was more money coming back here, so the younger crowd hadn't to go.

The annual cycle of farm work meant that people could spend the later part of winter and the spring in Donegal, preparing ground and planting their own crops, and then leave in midsummer to work on Scottish farms. The move to industrial work, accelerated by the war, upset this pattern:

> The majority of the people would be back before Saint Patrick's Day, to cultivate the land and cut the turf … and away again in the month of June … In the olden days … once the shouing [turnip harvesting] was done on a farm [in Scotland] – that would be December or February, the farmer didn't want them until the singling of the turnips … And that would be in the month of June, you see. That suited the man round here.

However, if a man had industrial work in England or Scotland, and left it to return to Donegal for spring farmwork, he would have difficulty getting the job again on his return. This led many people to give up the attempt to maintain a smallholding in Donegal. After the outbreak of the Second World War, Hugh said, many people stopped coming back to Donegal, except for a fortnight's holiday each year.

The career of John Magennis, farm labourer

For urban people used to terms and conditions of employment in industry, the agricultural working arrangement that is easiest to understand is day labouring, where a farm worker was contracted to work on a weekly basis, carrying out agreed tasks for a number of hours, which at least theoretically were fixed.

The Lagan valley, running south-west from Belfast, has some of Ulster's oldest industrial centres, which first grew up with the linen industry in the later eighteenth century. Despite its predominantly rural character, industrial life is familiar to local families, many of whose members have worked in both sectors of the economy. John Magennis, who was born about one mile outside the town of Lurgan, came from such a family. His father was a telephone engineer, 'just ordinary working class'. John attended two schools in Lurgan, but left at the age of fourteen and a half. He started work as a farm labourer with the Upritchard family at Kilmore, about three miles from his home. He walked to and from the farm each day of a six-day week, starting work at 8 a.m. and finishing at 6 p.m.

The Upritchards' farm was 'medium' for the area, between seventy and eighty acres in extent. The farm was mixed, producing beef cattle, potatoes, barley, wheat and grass seed.

There were no women on the farm, which was run jointly by three brothers. One of these men did the household work, but John Magennis said that in general their practical involvement with the farming operation was limited.

There were three horses on the farm, and a man was employed specially to work with these. John Magennis, who had no previous experience with farming, learned to carry out manual tasks such as planting and harvesting potatoes and binding grass-seed by hand. He already knew a little about the work because he had watched farmers around his own home, but apart from this he 'just had to go and see what the rest was doing'. He stayed about three years on the farm, by which time he had learnt a lot. His increasing skills were not reflected in his pay, which remained at six shillings a week.

After leaving the Upritchards, John became a lorry driver. He taught himself to drive, and never took a driving test. His new employer was a local 'coal and sand' man:

> He was a … Lurgan man. He had three lorries, and … a sand pit down in Derryclone …
> It was all heavy work for a young fellow coming up on eighteen years of age …
> I drew sand to a big plant … outside Carrickfergus [at] Kilroot – shovelled it on
> with a navvy's shovel, and shovelled it off … there was no such thing as tipping
> gears then.

The major incentive to change from farming was the increase in his pay. His starting wage as a lorry driver was £2 a week. Also, hours were shorter, as he stopped work at lunchtime on Saturdays, and worked only until 5.30 p.m. during the week.

John stayed with this firm until the beginning of the Second World War, which produced a short-term but dramatic improvement in employment opportunities in the Lurgan area. His driving skills meant that he got work at Langford Lodge,[13] which was developed as an American base during the war. John drove diggers and dumpers, and also worked overtime, driving other workers to and from the site. His pay rose very sharply, and he sometimes took home £70 a week. His employers, Lockheed Overseas Corporation, were 'great' to work for. 'You'd no trouble with them at all. It was the ordinary Irish foreman, and it was just you were employed by the Americans … aw it was a great job, it was like Heaven!'

The work lasted almost eight years, but ended soon after the war, when the workers were paid off. John Magennis went to sign on at the Lurgan Employment Bureau, but he was unemployed for only one week. He heard of a new job through his wife Mary, whom he had married near the start of the war:

> The missus was working for a woman called Mrs Liddell, and her daughter was married
> to Mr Jordan, the big pig and cattle man. So it was through Mary I got the job. [Mr
> Jordan] said he would employ me for a month to see if I was worthy of the job … so I
> went down there and stayed for the month, and he told me, 'I'm going to keep you on'.
> I stayed thirty-nine years at it!

The Jordans' farm was very large by Ulster standards, and particularly for a farm specialising in pig production, which was generally linked to small holdings. John Magennis became one of the Jordans' key workers, eventually being given the title 'foreman'. His initial experiences, however, were in sharp contrast to the highly paid driving job he had had during the war, as he was employed as a semi-skilled labourer:

> The wages – you talk about a comedown! … four pound ten a week … And do you know what I was doing? I was going into the middle of a field along with another chap – into maybe 200 acres of ground, with a graip and a long-tailed shovel, and … spreading muck. You were a muck man, – that's all you could call yourself – pigs' muck.

Pigs' muck, which had to be cleaned out of houses as well as spread over fields, figured largely in John's work because of the scale of livestock farming carried on by the Jordans. When he started working there, he said that there were about a hundred Friesian bullocks kept for beef, and about 2,000 pigs. The pigs were fattened and brought in loads of about thirty-five a time to the firm of Denny, in Portadown. Crops were relatively unimportant, but oats, grass-seed, wheat and fodder crops were cultivated.

Under Mr Hercules Jordan's direction, and later that of his son Harry, the farming enterprise developed. According to John Magennis, the farm at Kilmore had 136 acres, but 'the thing … built up and built up … They bought Fortland in Aghalee, there was 110 acres in it. They bought Cherryvalley in Crumlin, that was 460 [300] acres there.[14] They bought Dromore, there was another 300 [180] acres there.' The farms were all within a radius of about fifteen miles of one another. John estimated that about 110 cattle were kept at Fortland, 500 [300] bullocks at Cherryvalley, 180 heifers and two bulls at Dromore, and up to 400 cattle at Kilmore. When he left his job, more than 40,000 [25,000] pigs were kept for fattening. Pigs were bought when they were about sixteen weeks and fattened at the rate of six to seven pounds per week. John Magennis became very expert in the care and management of pigs. He said that he learnt a lot from the vet who came to the farm:

> Whenever he came to Jordans' to do anything, he would have showed you … how to do the thing. So I kept my eye on him all the time, what he was doing. If I wanted to know anything, I'd have asked him … He told me everything.

John was particularly skilful in identifying sick pigs, and pigs that were ready for sale:

> Whenever I went to the yard in the mornings … [the first thing I'd do was] take a syringe … and bottles of penicillin [carried around my waist] … The syringe held thirty CCs. And I'd to go round every pig house … and if a pig was bad, I just injected it in the house – say it needed five CCs.

Pigs were kept in 'sweat boxes' designed to keep fat down. Some of these houses held up to 300 [75] animals. When John first went to the farm, every pig had to be pulled out and put on a weighbridge. After about six months' working experience, however, John found that he could go into a pig house with a pair of clippers and nick the ear of any pig he considered ready for slaughtering, without any weighing. He claimed that he became accurate in guessing a pig's weight to within two or three pounds.

John said that the Jordans were always in the lead in technological change. Within a year of his arrival on the farm, tractors replaced horses; methods of ventilating and feeding pigs were changed radically several times. In John's early days on the farm, pigs were fed simply by throwing meal on to the floor of each house, but by the time he left a system had been installed that enabled 12,000 pigs to be fed in half an hour. The disposal of pig waste changed from the slow, laborious method of carting and spreading by hand to a 'bizzer' that sprayed the slurry over the field. This in turn was replaced by a piped system. Three and a half [$^1/_2$ to $^3/_4$] miles of aluminium pipes distributed the waste throughout the farm, the waste being driven along by an 80–90 HP engine.

John said that there was a considerable turnover of staff on the Jordans' farms, but he estimated that at any time there was a workforce of about nine labourers. Four of the men employed were based at Kilmore, and for a period two men, Pat McAlernon and his son, lived and worked at the Cherryvalley farm, receiving wages and the use of the farm house rent-free. A number of labourers were based at the family's other farms. The workers were given titles – for example, tractor man, lorryman and foreman – but John said that the division of labour was not rigid. 'You just gave a hand at everything.' Workers moved from farm to farm as required. Although Pat McAlernon and his son were based at Cherryvalley, 'that doesn't say they were running it. All they [did] was the pigs … [The Kilmore workers] had to go down and do the cattle … and pump out the muck for them.' James Jordan, the son of Hercules and brother of Harry, lived on a farm at Drumban, and three Kilmore workers were sent there each Monday morning to 'pull out' the pigs ready for slaughter. In the later period of John's employment, up to 900 pigs were sent away each week.

Relationships between John Magennis and the Jordans were friendly, and characterised by straight, often blunt, talking. John described an incident that occurred between himself and Hercules Jordan that shows this clearly. The Jordans usually provided food for their labourers only if they were working late at harvest time, and this usually consisted of tea, bread and jam. One morning, some time after John had started work at Kilmore, he arrived at the farm late:

> I landed down and the first man I met was [Hercules] … He says, 'This is a time to be starting your work … They're near finished.' Says I, 'The wife wasn't too well … Things is not just right.' 'Go on with your work!' – He scared the heart out of me … [However,] ten minutes after that, I could hear him shouting, 'John! Come in! Mammy has something for you' – that was his missus. So I goes in. Two eggs, bacon, sausages, dipped bread, tea and all! And I ate every bite, for I hadn't got anything [at home]. And he had a sausage left himself, and a bit of bacon. 'Put that into you too, for I can't eat it, don't waste it.' And whenever I was putting the last bite into my mouth, he gave a gulder out of him … He scared the living daylights out of me! 'Get away back to your work!' – But it was decent.

Hercules' son Harry took over the running of the farm about two years after John Magennis started work there. Relationships between Harry and John were also expressed in a forthright way. John addressed Harry Jordan by his Christian name, and his manner was not at all deferential:

> I happened to come in this morning, whatever happened – my back was sore or something, and I was five minutes late. And he [Harry Jordan] was passing me by [and he looked at his watch] … Says I, 'What are you looking at? Do you want to know the time?' Says I, 'It's near ten past eight'. 'Aye,' he says, 'You're showing a bad example to the rest John, on account of being as long here.' Says I, 'Away in … and get your breakfast … and quit talking … and give my head a minute's peace!'

Probably because of this mutual directness, John Magennis said that Harry Jordan and he 'got on very well together'. John and his wife Mary went regularly to the Jordans' house at night to baby-sit the three children if Harry Jordan and his wife were going out, for example, to a special night at the golf club. John was especially fond of one of the Jordan girls, Eleanor, with whom, he said, he was 'the best of friends'.

By the time John left the farm his pay had risen to £80 a week. He had to retire early after an accident:

> It was one of the big [double] gates … into the silage pit. It was about [12 feet wide on each side]. And the two [gates] met together with a big bar … [which] went across and held them … I saw it two or three times now, fellows nearly getting their legs off, because the gate was … [about] a foot off the ground, and [with] … the wind catching it, you couldn't have held it. It was my Sunday on [and I was getting ready for it]. I says to Tim Haughey [another worker] … 'Tim, cut a bit off that cover for silage, for I'm not coming in here on a Sunday morning to take covers off silage pits!' So we got the thing trailed off … and just as we were ready to go, the pin shot out of the ground – broke the cement, and [the gate] went back full blast. And you know the part you hold in your hand … for putting the big bar across – I was behind that, and that hit me off [a] wall, and I [had to get] … my head stitched right across … and I got my heart damaged.

After this incident, John retired, and he and wife lived in a small house near Lurgan.

The case studies above suggest that the degree of formality in the relationship between farmers and labourers could vary greatly. An observation made in 1947 by John M. Mogey relates these differences to farm size:

> On … tiny farms there is little difference in wealth between labourer and farmer and social distinctions, while not absent, are very slight. In districts where the average farm size is over 30 acres such social distinctions become more marked. Farmer and labourer still work in the fields together as in other regions, but often they separate on returning to the farm house. The master eats his meal in a separate room from the labourer: these

are the farm houses of two kitchens, a front kitchen for the family and a back kitchen for
the workers and domestic servant. Prosperity, and where it is not yet present, the social
drive towards the amassing of material possessions, would seem to put a barrier between
master and man. This tendency is inherent in the structure of rural society.[15]

However, the case studies also show that we must be careful not to make too direct a link
between working relationships and farm size. The terms and conditions under which workers
like John Magennis was employed probably come as near to urban arrangements as was
possible on a farm. However, even here we can see that there are differences between industrial
and agricultural work, and these seem to relate to the amount of personal contact between
employer and employee, and the level of interest that employees took in the operation of the
business. These differences can be understood by the continuing close interaction between
farmer and workers necessary on most farms, and the creative element built into much farm
work. The production of a fine crop, or even more obviously the breeding and the care of
young animals, engages the attention much more directly than the limited number of tasks
allocated to workers employed in the mass production of industrial and high-tech
commodities. Organisers of labour movements generally pointed to the relative isolation of
farm workers as a difficulty in getting them to join unions, or to take joint action to improve
conditions, but it is probably also the case that the engagement of many workers with their
work meant a relative lack of alienation from the production process.

7. Recent history

The introduction to this book emphasises the extent to which modernisation has reduced regional diversity. This is a sad loss, but local character often coexisted with shocking levels of poverty. The hardship of many people's lives even after the Second World War was clearly documented by John Mogey in 1947. His account of rural life in County Fermanagh[1] shows how bad things could be.

Only between 11% and 16% of farms in County Fermanagh were regarded as economically viable. In a case study of the area around the small town of Lisbellaw, Mogey found that only 10% of houses had piped water. Even in the town, many houses had only a tap at the back door, and residents used a stand-pipe in the main street. In some poorer rural districts whole townlands were without even a well, and, surprisingly for such a wet and unspoilt place, in some ill-drained areas of clay land the water had to be boiled before it was drunk. In these instances, Mogey commented, 'Tea reverts to its original purpose of a disguise for the flavour of boiled water'. Half of the houses in rural Fermanagh as a whole had no source of water within 100 yards, and 96% of houses had no running water. Around 70% of houses had no lavatory of any kind, and 96% of all houses had neither gas nor electricity supplies for cooking or lighting.[2] It was rural poverty such as this that led to the development in both the North and the South of Ireland of notions of planned economic development, based on significant government intervention.

As we have seen, the Second World War confirmed the view that the government had an important role in supporting the agricultural sector, and in planning its direction. The forty years that followed the war will probably be looked back on as a period when centralised government planning of many aspects of life was seen as progressive and efficient. Health, education, housing and transport were some of the sectors where the state developed planning strategies, which were assumed to be essential to efficiency and well-being. Attempts at planning agricultural production were part of a much wider movement.

Apologists for state intervention of this kind presented it as essentially benign, but this was not how many country people perceived it. In the divided world of Northern Irish politics, we might expect suspicion of state activities to be prevalent among Nationalists, but Rosemary Harris found that around Ballygawley in County Tyrone during the 1950s, suspicion of officialdom was widespread among both Unionists and Nationalists. 'Most farmers believed that the Ministry of Agriculture was not merely occasionally unwise or genuinely mistaken but had no real desire to help them.'[3]

Harris convincingly relates this to the lack of trust country people had in impersonal procedures:

There was distrust and dislike of the officials who came into the area enforcing rules about health, about schooling, and about the running of farms … In part much irritation … stemmed from the failure of local people to comprehend the impersonal attitudes of bureaucracy. Local relationships were always on a face-to-face basis, and were largely with people known as individuals in a number of different contexts. It was not surprising that the people did not believe that the decisions of officials were reached in accordance with the demands of impersonal rules.[4]

This suspicion illustrates very well the tensions between local, small-scale culture and the anonymity of globalising modernity. However, the state's approach to agricultural planning did achieve a lot in reducing rural poverty, and in giving farmers with viable holdings a period of economic security. This was approvingly summarised in 1963:

Since the war … market stability has been achieved by the establishment of assured markets and guaranteed prices … have been maintained for fat cattle, fat sheep and fat pigs, liquid milk, wool, eggs, potatoes and cereals. Other important products of Ulster farms, such as store cattle and store sheep, have received good prices because the end products have had an assured market. Preparation of farms for long-term efficiency has been encouraged by generous grants and subsidies.[5]

Fig. 39 Allister McQuoid, aged two, on Beattie's farm near Kilmore County Down in 1957. In 1982 Allister was awarded a Ph.D in Astrophysics from Queen's University Belfast and by 1987 had gained a M.Sc. in Business Management from the prestigious Massachusetts Institute of Technology Boston USA. He is also an internationally respected mountaineer. During an expedition to the Peruvian Andes in 1980, he made ascents of Nevado Ulta (5875 metres altitude) by the North East Ridge, the first ever ascent of this climb, and Artesonraju (6025 metres) by the East Ridge and South Face.

Between the early 1930s and 1960 there was an overall rise in agricultural prices, and the period can be seen as one of relative economic security for farmers.[6]

In the decades following 1960, however, radical changes occurred in farming methods, the organisation of the agricultural sector of the economy, patterns of international trade, and the way in which farming and the people engaged in it were seen by the public. The large-scale success in increasing production and raising standards of living was accompanied by large-scale difficulties. Overproduction led to the notorious growth of European 'food mountains', while intensive arable farming led to massive environmental destruction, including pollution of water, the uprooting of hedgerows, and the negative effects of monoculture on biodiversity. The development of intensive livestock farming methods was widely seen as cruel, and also as making meat products unsafe, resulting in terrifying health risks, most notoriously BSE (*bovine spongiform encephalopathy* – 'mad cow disease') and the foot and mouth epidemic, which affected a number of Ulster farms in 2001. Urban people's view of farmers changed radically during all of these changes. The view of country people as quaint 'folk' who lived in age-old harmony with nature often gave way to stereotypes of farmers as ruthless, ignorant destroyers of beneficent nature.

Farming people see this view as extremely unfair. The withdrawal of the economic security ensured by legislation such as the EEL Common Agricultural Policy meant that by the end of the twentieth century many farmers were facing great, and in some cases insurmountable, financial problems. Farmers' attitude to farming their holdings remains as pragmatic as it appears always to have been, but it is nonsense to see this as implying a lack of care for the land. Farmers in general are well aware that the long-term well-being of farming is directly related to the long-term health of the environment. Shortsighted greed is a common human failing. It is not more common among farmers than anyone else.

Many of the people whose testimonies provide the main evidence used in writing this book are no longer engaged in farming, and some no longer live on farms. Country people have increasingly taken advantage of the new opportunities for careers away from the family farm, some of them travelling very far (and indeed very high!) (Fig. 39). Agriculture remains one of the staple industries of Ulster, but it is carried on by a dramatically decreasing rural population.

We can make some generalisations about the kinds of people most likely to leave. In Ireland as a whole, for at least a century, many more women have left farming than men.[7] In recent decades, at least some women have always had to find work outside farming. The new conditions, which they saw as encouraging them to go in the mid-twentieth century, were the decreasing need for labour on farms and the widening opportunities to do other things. As we have also seen, the deskilling of farm women, and the subsequent possibility of loss of status, have been suggested as an explanation for this Europe-wide phenomenon. Farm women who have stayed on the land have developed new interests, including the book-keeping aspects of farming, local non-agricultural work, and community activities.[8] The influences shaping women's decisions have also applied to large numbers of men.

There has been an ongoing acceptance that many people would have to leave the land, and a growing awareness of possibilities elsewhere.

The following summaries give an indication of some of the necessities, and strategies, that shaped the choices of people in recent decades.

In Ireland generally, emigration was one of the most brutal routes taken by people leaving their family farms. During the twentieth century this was most drastic in the west. Hugh Ward's account of the depopulation of Keadew on Donegal's Atlantic coast describes the situation prevailing in many western areas. Permanent emigration from Keadew was high until the 1960s. One of Hugh's sisters moved to Nottingham, and a brother, who for some time had his own farm in Donegal, eventually settled permanently in Glasgow. Two other brothers went to America as young men. One became a policeman in Detroit, the other a factory worker in New York:

> They used to have what they called the convoys here – that was the night before they went to America … They'd be sitting up all night till morning, singing and what-not. All sorrowful songs. And crying – some of them crying. Then they would all leave the house in the morning to catch the nine o'clock train at Castleroad station … and they were all walking on maybe four abreast …
>
> Some of them came back, and some didn't. My brother [who went to New York] was forty years away before he came back. My father and mother was dead before he came back … The old lad used to write to him, and tell him to come … and he said he would like to come, but the thought of going back again for the last time … he thought he couldn't stand up to that. The last letter I got from him before he died, he said if he could make it at all the following spring … that he was going to come … he wanted to die in Ireland. But he never made it.

Hugh's father died in 1952. Hugh stayed on the family farm until 1962, with his wife and daughter, but finally moved permanently to Carlisle. At that time, 'you would go outside here, and you wouldn't see a light'. The Keadew area was almost entirely depopulated. Hugh had made a living working on the farm and by doing work for the local council. He had also been working for several summers in Carlisle, however, and had made contacts that made it fairly easy for him to find permanent work in England. Ironically, within three years of the family leaving, fish factories were set up around the nearby town of Burtonport and more local work became available. This work attracted some people back to the area, and during the 1970s and 1980s new houses were built in considerable numbers. One of Hugh Ward's daughters moved back to Keadew with her husband and children in the 1980s, and Hugh also moved back after his retirement, living in his family home until his death in 2002.

In more affluent farming areas, possibilities for change could be as important in shaping decisions as economic necessities. The increasing opportunities provided by education had a major influence here. On the Murphys' farm near Hilltown, for example, the children were well grown by the late 1920s and some of the older children were leaving home to follow a variety of careers. One of the daughters, Gertie, became a priest's housekeeper, while Mary Kate eventually became headmistress of a local primary school. Rose settled nearby in Hilltown. Another daughter, Delia, married a businessman who also farmed, while another, Lil-Anne, went to live in Connemara, where she worked as a nurse and midwife. Eddie and Dan, Mary Catherine Murphy's eldest sons, followed their half-brothers to California, where Dan became a policeman. Frank, the third eldest, also left the farm, around 1930. He and his youngest brother Joey were educated at the Abbey school in Newry; after successfully taking their 'Senior' exams, they went to Greenmount College, outside Antrim. In 1935, Joey was one of twelve students awarded a scholarship to Greenmount College, by the Down Committee of Agriculture.[9]

After college, Frank found work as a food inspector with the Irish Department of Agriculture, first in County Louth and later in County Sligo, where he married and settled, raising a family of six children. Joey Murphy was employed by the Northern Ireland Ministry of Agriculture, and worked for several years around Lisnaskea in County Fermanagh. He had to leave this job because of bad health. He returned to County Down and found work in Banbridge, with a road contractor. Here he met his wife Jane, whom he married in 1954. The two remaining sons, John and Peter Owen, stayed on the family farm, which John eventually inherited in 1946 on the death of his mother. After 1976 the farm was let out in conacre.

By 1989, Peter Owen was the last of the Murphy children to remain alive. He stayed in the family house, but the farm's land was sold in 1983 following the death of John's wife, Clare.

Although the family farm no longer operates, the family history is obviously not one of sad decline. In the present generation, members of the Murphy family live in many parts of Ireland and America, taking advantage of an even wider range of educational and career opportunities than was available to their parents.

Not all the skills that could be developed by farming people were new, or meant leaving the local area. In the period studied, the local economy provided outlets other than farming. Two of the Lyons sisters, living on their farm in Gannoway, County Down, got local jobs – Netta as a shop assistant and Dolly as a dressmaker. In the Cloverhill area of County Cavan, Bob Lee took advantage of local markets for farm carts and spade shafts. Bob's father was a gifted joiner, and specialised in making the bodies of carts. Bob became interested in woodwork while still very young. He attempted his first very difficult task when a wheel on one of the family's carts was broken. The cart was temporarily abandoned, and when the family went to recover it, they found that the other wheel had been stolen. Bob offered to make new wheels for the cart; although sceptical, his father let him try. The project was a success, and Bob began to make carts for sale. His woodworking activities developed until in 1937 he opened a sawmill half a mile from Ballyhaise Railway Station and seven miles from Cavan town. He usually employed one or two workmen in the mill, sawing timber and building farm carts and barrows. The mill also produced scythe handles

Fig. 40 Corn harvest at Kilkeel, County Down. From left to right: Rose Forsythe, John Forsythe, Lily Park, Sam Park, William Quinn, John Park and two unknown people (photograph courtesy of Mr Gilbert Patterson (UFTM L283/6))

and spade shafts, the latter in very large quantities. The well-known McMahon's spademill in Clones, County Monaghan, provided him with orders of up to 'one hundred dozen' spade shafts in a single batch.

Bob Lee moved to Lambeg, County Antrim in 1958. He continued working at making carts and fine horse-drawn vehicles right up to his death in the spring of 1990.

In County Fermanagh, Joe Kane took jobs away from the farm at Drumkeeran for as long as his uncle was active, but eventually stopped, 'to stay at home to look after him when he got aged. I was left with him from I was seven year old, and then I'd have been very ungrateful if I'd went away and left him … in his old age.' After his uncle died, Joe once again went to work outside the farm. 'You couldn't make a living from the farm, it was that small.' He worked on several state schemes, and eventually took a job with the forestry service, where he stayed for nine years until his retirement. This work included making drains, cutting hedges, and felling timber. He remained on his farm in Drumkeeran until the 1990s, 'one of the few residents in the townland, and the oldest surviving one'. Depopulation meant that by the 1990s there were only three families in the townland. Joe's last job included assisting in the demolition of neighbours' farms and integrating them into coniferous plantations.

The decline in farming as a way of life may or may not continue. A common strategy for small farmers in many parts of the world has been to keep a foothold in the land, which can provide security for the family in times of hardship or insecurity.[10] Only the future will show whether this remains a viable strategy for farming people in Ireland.

It was pointed out at the start of this book that the period covered is one commonly seen in terms of the massive movements of modernisation, and it may be that these changes have made a return to an economy of small family-run farms increasingly unlikely. Commentators who see modernisation as progress, but also those who lament the apparently inexorable destruction of old ways that it often brings, agree that in the late twentieth century farming people's way of life changed radically, undermining many previously held certainties. However, the overwhelming conclusion to be drawn from the testimonies included here is an optimistic one, and the repetition of an age-old lesson. No matter how tough, or seemingly sterile, conditions might appear at the macro-level, human experience remains determinedly and exuberantly rich (Fig. 40).

8. Oral testimony as history

The history presented in this book has attempted to link personal experiences with large-scale economic and social movements. It is clear that the material presented has been taken mostly from oral testimonies, and it seems appropriate to end the book with a discussion of the potential of the oral history method, but also the particular problems raised by it. The following account relies heavily on Gaynor Kavanagh's work on the subject. Anyone interested in learning more about modern thinking on memory and oral testimony, and the construction of personal and public histories using these, is recommended to begin with her book *Dream Spaces: Memory and the Museum.*[1]

How we remember

Kavanagh emphasises that memory is not just one aspect of our lives, which we can refer to or not, at will. Our memories are fundamental to our sense of ourselves. Susan Greenfield argues that memory is not an 'add-on brain accessory but a cornerstone of holistic and cohesive consciousness'. Our memories are us, and they come in many forms.[2] 'We are making ourselves as much as making a record of the past when we bring things to mind. This is as evident in what we forget as what we remember.'[3]

We can understand just how essential memory is when we consider even the most routine activities. How would we get home if we had no memory, or how would we cook a meal? As Greenfield argues, however, memory also works at much deeper levels than this, giving us the fundamental sense of who we are, and what our personality is.

Kavanagh points out that when we recall the past, we go through a process, which can be helped by prompts that stimulate the senses. We all know that memory can be triggered by cues such as old songs, photographs, or smells. How we are feeling can also lead us to bring different memories to our conscious minds. People can be encouraged to remember in environments where reflection is safe or even unavoidable,[4] and the people to whom we are recounting our memories are also of profound importance. Equally clearly, however, these situations in which memories are shared can also lead to the suppression or restructuring of what is remembered, both intentionally and unintentionally. For Eric Hobsbawm, this is the most urgent issue to be faced in oral history: 'Most oral history today is personal memory, which is a remarkably slippery medium for preserving facts … memory is not so much a recording as a selective mechanism, and the selection is, within limits, constantly changing.'[5]

Suppression and restructuring can happen at any time between the historical event and the time at which they are presented as testimony. Researchers have become increasingly interested in recording such changes, and attempting to understand what has led to them. It is obvious that people sometimes deliberately falsify their accounts of the past in situations where they feel it is important to keep some parts of it secret, but apart from this, there are well-documented instances where memories recorded as oral testimonies have been unintentionally restructured to such an extent that they bear very little resemblance to events recorded in written records made at the time.

One well-known example has been recorded in England. A woman interviewed about her memories of the declaration of the Second World War recounted that, 'We were all together in our little living room … [the family] all together for once', when Neville Chamberlain made his historic radio broadcast. She remembered that they were all 'shaken to the roots' by the first siren alert. However, a documentary account that she had written at the time, and which came to light later, described a very different situation. She had not heard the broadcast, or the siren, but was playing the piano when her mother burst in shouting at her, and her father came in issuing orders and useless advice![6] In another case study, David Thelen, examining memories of the Watergate scandal in the USA, found that people not only restructured their own memories but also negotiated the content of these memories through discussion with others, allowing them to shape their recollections, so that they refashioned not only their accounts of the past but even what they actually remembered, to please the people with whom they were discussing it.[7]

Many scholars now recognise that memories are constructed rather than simply recounted, and that making oral history from these memories is not simply a case of tapping into the deep, undisturbed well of knowledge that people carry inside their heads. They have become interested in investigating not only the relationship between the interviewer and the person interviewed, or how memories have been distorted by intervening exchanges with other people, but also the narrative structure used by people in structuring their memories.[8]

People do not usually organise their memories using the principles of academic discipline. In oral history we often deal with the kind of data produced by what has been described as 'episodic memory': long-term memories called up when we remember events, places and people within the terms of our lives. Unless we rehearse our memories regularly, we do not call them up sequentially, but as episodes hinged to important events. These may be major public events, such as before, after, or during 'the war' or 'the Troubles'. They may be important events in our personal lives, such as when we started work, or had our first date. People also fix events by relating the episodes to rites of passage within their own lives or those of their family, such as births, marriages and deaths.[9] All of these types of memory marker can be clearly seen in the testimonies on which this book has been built up. We have seen, for example, that the Second World War had profound effects on farming, as did technical advances such as electrification and the introduction of tractors, while life events, such as the date when someone was married or when their mother died, were used to place other memories in a historical context.

Despite the filtering and refracting of memories, with subsequent distortions in testimony produced by personal and social pressures and the conventions of communication, the overwhelming characteristic of oral evidence is its richness as a historical source. Historical episodes that have been recorded in manuscripts or printed documents usually require a lot of imaginative speculation from researchers attempting to identify the aims and motives of the people whose activities are described. This applies most obviously to statistical records, which record the results of activities but not the strategies that underlay them, or the ironies and contradictions arising from the unintended consequences of action. Collecting oral testimonies, on the other hand, allows us to explore people's memories of the goals and feelings that led them to take particular actions. Most obviously, oral testimonies provide evidence of aspects of the past that have never been previously recorded and are simply not accessible in any other way, the level of detail available being limited only by the power of recall of the person interviewed and the time and energy of the collector.

Fieldwork techniques

Given the above, it is clear that in oral history fieldwork, the relationship between the interviewer and the person being interviewed is of central importance. This means that attempting to describe best practice for approaches to fieldwork can only be of limited value. In the end it is impossible to discuss the interaction between people analytically. Human communication is so subtle that the most adequate expressions of it are probably found in the arts, rather than in reductionist academic texts. The following are therefore only rough guidelines that are important to bear in mind:

> There are tried and tested ways of working which aid the interviewer and structure the interview so that the informant is assisted in recall and recollection. Questions that gently progress from the factual to the analytical allow the keying in of memory, the tumbling of recollections and the reflection on them, one after another. Different forms of questions, in particular – open rather than closed – and the minimum of interviewer intervention can promote the freer expression of thoughts and descriptions. Beyond doubt, the interviewer's knowledge of the subject and from that the ability not only to relate to what is being said, but also to move the topic both forward and deeper through appropriate use of terms or questions which are apposite are important.[10]

The following six rules on listening were suggested by Michael Jacobs in 1985:

1. Listening requires giving full attention, without interrupting.
2. Do not change the subject unnecessarily.
3. Listen to the bass line of what is being said. (This refers to emotional issues that might emerge during interviews.)

4. Listen to what people are not saying and respect that silence.
5. Listen to the body language of the person being interviewed.
6. In responding, use questions to prompt, link and explore.[11]

The mechanics of interviewing, using either a tape recorder, or increasingly, video recorders, are easily learnt and are in fact becoming easier as machines get smaller and more user-friendly. In general it is recommended that recording devices be kept in as unobtrusive a position as possible. However, sometimes people respond well to impressive machinery, which emphasises how important the interview is to the person and/or the institution making it.

Interviewing is the exciting part of oral history. The grinding slog comes afterwards, when the contents of tapes are transcribed. Best practice is that every word, every pause, and every interruption should be included in the manuscript record. In transcribing tapes used in this book, we estimated that every hour of taped conversation took twelve hours to document. It is best if the people who undertook the interview also carry out the transcription work. Anyone not well informed about the subject area covered in the tapes is liable to miss key points, and may even have difficulty following technical descriptions, especially if these are recounted in an unfamiliar dialect. Given this labour-intensive work, it is easy to understand why many oral history projects in the 1980s and 1990s fizzled out, with tapes left neglected on the shelves of libraries and community halls.

Assessing the evidence

One of the most important achievements of western thought is the rigorous, sceptical testing of evidence. This is as true for history as for any other field of academic study. The situation for historians is well summarised by Hobsbawm:

> The point from which historians must start, however far from it they may end, is the fundamental and, for them, absolutely central distinction between establishable fact and fiction, between historical statements based on evidence and subject to evidence and those which are not.
>
> It has become fashionable in recent decades … to deny that objective reality is accessible, since what we call 'facts' exist only as a function of prior concepts and problems formulated in terms of these. The past we study is only a construct of our minds …
>
> I believe that without the distinction between what is and what is not, there can be no history … Either Elvis Presley is dead or he isn't.[12]

In attempting to assess the data presented in oral testimonies, we should look for independent corroboration of the evidence. Comparison between oral evidence and contemporary documentary records, if they are available, is one of the best ways in which we can test the factual reliability of the oral accounts and put them in a wider context. Contemporary records, whether large-scale, such as census returns, or personal records such as diaries, can allow information such as dates or places to be cross-checked. This is especially important when oral evidence deals with material outside the direct experience of the person being interviewed:

> Outside of the principal periods within living memory, namely the stretch of, say, three to five generations, we can only catch occasional glimpses of the operation of oral testimony and transmissive practices within most literate societies … The personal account is the least likely testimony to survive.[13]

Where documentation is not available, different oral accounts of the same event can also sometimes be compared for consistency. Often, however, we have to rely on less direct approaches, such as checking for internal consistency in the details given within one testimony.

It has frequently been pointed out that oral testimonies tell us as much about the present views and experience of the person interviewed as about the past that they are describing. This does not put oral history in a unique place, however. Very few written accounts of the kind used by historians can be said to be contemporaneous with the events they describe, and these therefore are the same synthesis of descriptions of reality coloured by current interests that is so marked in oral testimony. Gaynor Kavanagh summarises the position of history in general:

> There are endless versions of the same event. The work of historians … is evidence of this. The presence of contradictory accounts can demonstrate that the things which are remembered, what is included and excluded, the words that are used, the allusions drawn, may be as relevant as the actual content. A person may indicate as much about themselves and their life experiences in what they do not say as in what they do.[14]

Empirical research is central to history. There have been great historical theories, but researching any particular period requires amassing as many pieces of empirical data as possible and testing their reliability.

The other great challenge in oral history research is to assess the data's significance, and how they might be linked in our understanding of the wider historical issues we are investigating. It is important to distinguish the two historical tasks. The past was real, and we can hope to find out what happened then, but its meaning changes. The philosopher Jean-Paul Sartre argued that historical knowledge, like all knowledge, is constantly changing its meaning.[15] We can understand this by a banal historical example. If I forget to buy a lottery ticket, my initial reaction may be one of frustration. Once the results of the lottery draw come out, however, I am much more likely to feel pleased that I saved my money! The historical fact of my forgetfulness is still there, but its meaning has been changed.

Despite the ever-changing meanings that we give to the past, however, we have a human obligation to try to understand it in as much complexity as we can. As Sartre has argued, the best historical account is one that, from our own point of view, we cannot go beyond.[16]

We have taken as many pieces of evidence as possible into account, tested the validity of these as rigorously as possible, and tried to assess their significance with as much intelligence and imagination as possible. This is as much as we can ever hope to achieve in historical understanding.

Ethics of collecting oral testimonies

There has been some discussion among historians, and within museums, about ethical issues involved in collecting oral evidence. A concern that people recorded for oral history archives are being exploited is central to the discussion.

As with collecting anything, recording testimonies is about taking something from people. 'No matter how well done and how thoughtfully organised, the basic motive is about appropriation.'[17] There is no doubt that people are very often unaware of the range of uses, some of them unacceptable, to which their testimonies might be put in the future.

A skilled interviewer can create such a relaxed atmosphere during the recording session that the person being recorded will behave simply as if they are having an intimate conversation with a friend. However, once the tape is deposited in an archive, it may be used many years later by people who have had no contact with the person giving the testimony, and who have a very wide range of agendas. It is the responsibility of the interviewer to make this clear before the recording is made, and to make sure that appropriate restrictions on access are documented.

However, it would be wrong to see the recording of oral history as only a product of hard-nosed calculation on the part of interviewers. It does not require great sensitivity for researchers to feel gratitude towards, and respect for, the people whose testimonies they record, particularly when they share an interest in, and some knowledge of, the aspects of life discussed. Also, many people interviewed welcome an opportunity to bear witness to their experiences, and see it as an affirmation of the value of their lives.

Even the experience of being interviewed can boost the social status of the person recorded. A very clear instance of this arose when we were collecting material for the present work. One of the people we recorded was the late Joe Kane, from Drumkeeran near Ederney, County Fermanagh. Mervyn Watson and myself were advised to contact Joe in the early 1980s by a colleague who had stopped to look at Joe's house in Drumkeeran, which had one of the few thatched roofs left in the area. It quickly became obvious that Joe was one of the best-informed people we had ever met. The long recording sessions that we organised with him attracted local attention. At that time, Mervyn Watson drove a 2CV, a slightly unusual car in the Ulster countryside, which was clearly visible on the hilly lane outside Joe's house. On our third visit, we were talking to Joe when two heads peeped round the open front door. They disappeared and came back, and eventually three local lads appeared, country-shy and country-satirical at the same time. They came in and sat on a bench along one wall, obviously impressed with the expensive recording equipment sitting on the earth floor of the room. One of Joe Kane's many great qualities was his modesty, but his pleasure at being seen as the centre of outsiders' attention was obvious. The lads disappeared after about half an hour, but we concluded that Joe's status as a local celebrity had been significantly increased, and in the years following we had the pleasure of sending a number of researchers to see Joe, who received them all with inimitable grace and courtesy. For us, this represented the task of collecting at its best. Joe Kane enjoyed it, we experienced the excitement of recording material that we found amazing, and the museum's archive was enriched by testimonies about the lives of Ulster people, bearing witness to their value and importance.

Appendix 1

People and farms included in the survey

This book is the result of fieldwork spanning more than two decades. Many people's testimonies were used, but some were recorded specially for the work. The following summarises basic data relating to some of the people whose testimonies were used as key pieces of evidence.

Dan J. McKay of Cookstown, Co. Tyrone (UFTM tape C77.55)
Dan McKay grew up on a farm of 28.5 acres about five miles outside Cookstown. His testimony is particularly useful in showing how neighbours negotiated terms under which co-operative working relationships might be established, or broken off.

Chapter
5 – The neighbours

John Drennan of Carse Hall, Ballykelly, Co. Derry (UFTM tape C77.116)
John Drennan's farm near Limavady was the wealthiest to be dealt with in detail in the book. The farm was laid out on newly reclaimed land along Lough Foyle during the mid-nineteenth century. It had more than 600 acres of arable land and a live-in work force of ten men; the family developed the largest livestock stud in Ireland.

Chapters
4 – Family farms
6 – Hired help

John A. Weir of Ballyroney, Co. Down (UFTM tape C78.54)
John Weir's testimony gives a clear description of the work of a small foundry in a rural area, particularly in showing how foundries responded to, and in some cases led, technological changes in their localities. Weir's foundry was established c. 1912, and manufactured and constructed ploughs, carts, barn fans, grubbers, and many small items such as cart stands.

Chapter
2 – Ulster farming, 1930–1960

Cormac McFadden, Dunfanaghy, Co. Donegal (UFTM tape R79.35)
Cormac McFadden grew up on a small farm in Roshin, north County Donegal, where the three arable acres were not enough to support the family. Cormac was hired locally as a boy, and his brothers worked in Scotland and the USA.

Chapters
5 – The neighbours

Mick McHugh of Hornhead, Co. Donegal (UFTM tape R81.115)
Mick McHugh lived all his life on the family farm at Hornhead. The family supplemented income from farming by a wide range of work, including fishing, horse-trading, joinery, migrant labour, and farm service. His testimony provides clear account of the diversity of tasks undertaken by farming families whose holdings were too small to work as independent commercial enterprises.

Chapters
5 – The neighbours
6 – Hired help

Pat McKillop of Moyarget, Co. Antrim (UFTM tape R81.141)

Pat McKillop worked as a blacksmith in a forge beside his home outside Ballycastle. His account is important in that it shows the role of blacksmiths as mediators between foundries and local farmers. The blacksmith was required to be familiar with the technicalities of both areas of work. Mr McKillop also explained how apparently simple farming operations could be used to express social tensions and conflicts.

Chapter
1 – Country people talking

James Ennis of Ballymoney, Co. Antrim (UFTM tape R84.85)

James Ennis, who later lived in the small market town of Ballymoney, County Antrim, spent much of his early life working as a hired man on several farms. James was born in Dublin in 1910. Both of his parents died while he was too young to remember, and he and his two brothers were sent to Nazareth Lodge children's home in Derry city. James stayed in the home until he was fourteen years old, at which point his guardians began to try to find him work. For some years after his time in farm service, James did casual work both locally and, on two consecutive summers, in south-west Scotland. In his early forties he found a job in a bacon factory, and worked there until he retired. He ended his life in a house near the centre of Ballymoney.

Chapter
6 – Hired help

Joe Kane of Drumkeeran, Co.Fermanagh (UFTM tapes R84.39, R84.40, R86.201 and R90.42)

Joe Kane was born in 1913 in the townland of Drumkeeran, about one mile north-west of the town of Ederney, County Fermanagh. During Joe's childhood there were eight families living in Drumkeeran, making up a population of about forty-five people. Farms in the area varied greatly in size. One large stock farm extended over more than 100 acres, while two other farms, which Joe Kane considered to have been commercially viable, were between thirty and forty acres in area. The smallest farms were between fourteen and seventeen acres, and were not self-supporting. Joe lived at first with his grandparents. His grandfather, who farmed one of the smallest holdings in the townland, also worked as a shoemaker. On the death of his grandparents Joe was sent, at the age of seven, to live with his uncle, John Kane. Joe remained on this holding for almost all of his life, inheriting it in 1953 when his uncle died at over ninety years of age.

Chapters
4 – Family farms
5 – The neighbours
6 – Hired help
7 – Recent history

Gerry McCormick of Monaghan town (UFTM tape R85.145)

Gerry McCormick's family settled near Rockcorry shortly after the Troubles of the early 1920s. Not only did the family buy a farm, but relatives opened businesses, including a pub, in Rockcorry. Gerry McCormick worked in Mona Creameries, Monaghan Town, where he eventually became manager. Mr McCormick's testimony gives a clear account of how a family that had been affected by political instability successfully established itself within an area.

Chapter
1 – Country people talking

Bob Lee of Cloverhill, Co. Cavan (UFTM tapes R86.268 and R86.269)

Cloverhill is about six miles from Cavan town, on the main road to Clones in County Monaghan. Bob Lee was one of six children born on a farm of around sixty acres, about half a mile from the demesne at Cloverhill. Mr Lee was born in 1912. His clearest memories of farming date from the 1920s. His testimony provides a very clear account of the workings of a mixed commercial farm in the Border area, and his own developing business in sawmilling and joinery.

Chapters
3 – Farm produce
4 – Family farms
5 – The neighbours
7 – Recent history

Hugh Paddy Óg Ward of Keadew, Co. Donegal (UFTM tape R87.60)

Hugh Paddy Óg Ward was born in 1910, one of eight children reared on a farm typical of many in the Rosses, in County Donegal. The farm, situated in Keadew townland, about three miles north of Burtonport, had seven acres of arable land and rights to common grazing on a sea meadow of eighteen acres which was jointly controlled by four families. The Wards, like most families in the Rosses and neighbouring Gweedore, supplemented their income by activities other than farming, and particularly by migrant labour.

Chapters
3 – Farm produce
5 – The neighbours
6 – Hired help
7 – Recent history

Mary Wilson of Townavanney, Co. Fermanagh (UFTM tape R87.62)

Townavanney is a townland on the northern shore of Lower Lough Erne, facing Boa island. The nearest small towns are Kesh, about eight miles to the east, and Belleek, about eleven miles to the west. Mrs Mary Wilson went to live on her husband's farm in the townland after her marriage in October 1937. Her husband, Thomas Wilson, had a farm of forty-two acres of fairly good land, and common grazing in a 'mountain' area of about one hundred and thirty acres that he shared with four other farmers. The Wilson family cut turf on Derrin mountain, about one and a half miles from Letter. Mrs Wilson's testimony gives a particularly clear account of a commercially viable farm in the west of Ulster, from a woman's perspective.

Chapters
3 – Farm produce
5 – The neighbours
6 – Hired help
7 – Recent history

Lily Cooke, Grace Montgomery and Ellen Gibson of Comber, Co. Down (UFTM tapes R87.90 and R87.91)

Mrs Lily Cooke and Mrs Grace Montgomery are sisters, who grew up on a farm in the townland of Lisbane. They, and a third sister, the late Mrs Teenie Magowan, helped their father, John Adams, with many of the tasks usually carried out by sons in a farming family. Mrs Ellen Gibson (née McClenaghan) also carried out a wide variety of tasks on her family's farm in the townland of Drumreagh. Both farms were commercially viable. The testimonies of the three women were recorded together, and provide a very valuable account of women's work on farms and in particular the co-operation between women in poultry farming.

Chapters
4 – Family farms
5 – The neighbours

Dolly McRoberts and Isabel Lyons of Gannoway, Co. Down (UFTM tape R87.163)

Dolly McRoberts and Isabel Lyons are sisters who grew up together on their family farm near Ballywalter, County Down. The farm was a small but commercially viable unit, where the four daughters carried out many of the tasks usually assigned to male family members. The women's testimonies give a particularly clear account of how skills were learnt by children within a very happy family.

Chapters
1 – Country people talking
4 – Family farms
7 – Recent history

Peter Owen Murphy of Mullaghmore, Co. Down (UFTM tape R89.54)

The Murphy family farmed in the townland of Mullaghmore near Hilltown, County Down, for two generations. The farm at Mullaghmore, or 'the Glen' as the area is known locally, included some good arable land and about fifty acres of mountain. The farmyard had a solid two-storey stone house, backed by an enclosed yard. The farm was mixed, but in this very distinctive area of hill country, the farming of sheep was of central importance. Peter Owen Murphy was one of three brothers active in running the farm from the 1920s.

Chapters
3 – Farm produce
7 – Recent history

Joe O'Neill of Dungiven, Co. Derry (UFTM tapes R89.118 and R89.119)

Joe O'Neill was born in Dungiven in 1919, the fifth in a family of nine children. His father, grandfather and great-uncle had all been butchers. A long yard behind the family house and (now converted) shop, on Dungiven's Main Street, had large sheds where cattle were tied for slaughtering. The O'Neills were also substantial farmers. They owned forty-five acres of good clay land in Derryware, a townland about a mile from Dungiven. There is no dwelling on this land, but it has a farmyard with a barn built over a shed, and stabling for horses. The O'Neills also rented land in conacre, especially during the Second World War, when tillage was greatly expanded. This is the only testimony included in the book that describes farming operations by a family whose main residence, and other sources of livelihood, were in a town.

Chapters
4 – Family farms
6 – Hired help

Malachy McSparran of Cloney, Co. Antrim (UFTM tapes R90.16 and R90.110)

Malachy McSparran's testimony is important in that it shows the slow accumulation of land by a family, over a number of generations, in an area of Ulster generally seen as having a particularly distinctive history. Documentation relating to the farm goes back to the 1790s, and shows the interchange between Antrim and Scotland, both economically and in the development of complex kinship ties. Mr McSparran describes an expanding pattern of mixed farming, which was not carried on very intensively in his grandfather's time but was developed by his father.

Chapters
1 – Country people talking
5 – The neighbours
7 – Recent history

John Magennis of Kilmore, Co. Armagh
John Magennis was born about one mile outside the town of Lurgan. He came from a family that made a living from both industry and farming, a fairly common situation in the Lagan Valley. His father was a telephone engineer, and Mr Magennis was clear that the family was working class. He attended two schools in Lurgan, but left at the age of fourteen and a half. He worked at both haulage and farm labouring. He went to work as a labourer on the Jordans' farm at Kilmore, where he worked for 39 years, eventually becoming farm foreman. His account describes the situation where farm labouring approached most closely to industrial working relationships, but also the important differences, particularly the closer relationships between employers and employees, and the engagement of workers with the content of their work.

Chapter
6 – Hired help

Bríd Coll of Gaoth Dobhair, Co. Donegal (UFTM tape R2000.99)
Bríd Coll is the only native Irish speaker whose testimony has been included in this book. Her family, like many in Gaoth Dobhair depended on the income earned by migrant work in Scotland, and hiring in Ulster. Bríd's account is particularly important in its description of her experience as a hired servant in her home area between the ages of 8 and 12, in Machaire Gathlán.

Chapter
6 – Hired help

Robert Strain of Rathfriland, Co. Down (UFTM tape R2001.72)
Robert Strain is an expert on local life in the Rathfriland district of County Down. The Ulster Folk and Transport Museum has many hours of interviews with Mr Strain, which deal with farming and commercial life around Rathfriland.

Chapter
2 – Ulster farming, 1930–1960

Mamie McQuoid and James McKeown of Kilmore, Co. Down (UFTM tape R2004.2)
Mrs McQuoid was reared in a house beside Ballynahinch Junction, County Down. Her father was a railway worker and her mother a dressmaker. James McKeown, her relative by marriage, had a family farm at Rademan, outside Kilmore village. They have clear memories of wartime conditions, including the impact of evacuees from Belfast on local life. Mrs McQuoid's children, Olga and Allister, also contributed to the account of their family history in more recent times.

Chapter
2 – Ulster farming, 1930–1960

Appendix 2

Some family photographs

Archie McSparran with his daughter Anne, and John 'Roi' Hamilton, at Cloney, Co. Antrim, in 1938

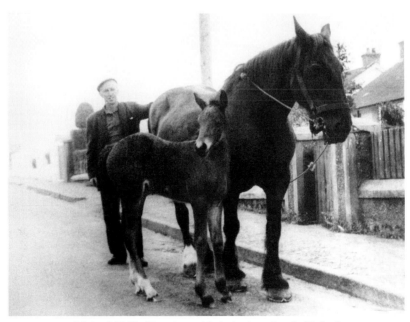

Mr Joe O'Neill of Dungiven, with the last horse kept by his family.
The foal became a show jumper in Italy (L3166/6)

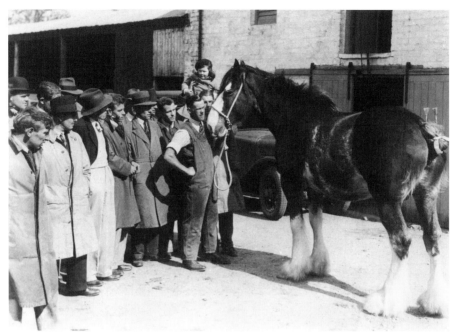

Mr Matt Drennan, John C Drennan's brother, with a Clydesdale from the Carse Hall stud
(photograph courtesy of Mr David Bigger and Mr Terry MacDonald)

Pat Doran of Ballymageogh, and his daughter, covering potatoes with a Mourne plough, near Attical,
County Down, in 1962 (L1864/5)

Hazlett Morrison working as a farm hand in Cogry, 1940

James McCluskey at Ballyclare Horse Fair in 1942

Frank and Joey Murphy of the Glen, Hilltown, with seed potatoes, in May 1931 (L2728/1)

William Lyons on his farm at Gannoway, County Down in the 1930s (L2726/4)

Tea in a field after cutting corn at Carrick East, Limavady. The woman is Lizzie Taylor, and the man beside her is hired help, Lesley Forrest. The man in the background is her father.

Mick Mullan ploughing the 18 acre field, O'Flynn's farm, Kircubbin c. 1952

Experimental spraying of potatoes in the 1930s

References

Introduction

1. Evans, E. Estyn. *The Personality of Ireland* (Dublin: Lilliput Press, 1992), p. 48.
2. Kavanagh, Patrick. *Collected Poems* (London: Martin Brian & O'Keeffe, 1972/1977), p. 30.
3. Hewitt, John. *The Day of the Corncrake* (Belfast: Glens of Antrim Historical Society, 1969), p. 10.
4. Ulster Folk and Transport Museum (UFTM) tape R81.115. Testimony of Mick McHugh, Hornhead, Co. Donegal.

Chapter 1: Country people talking

1. McSparran, Malachy. 'Growing up in the Glens'. Lecture presented to the Glens of Antrim Historical Society, 17 January 1997.

Chapter 2: Ulster farming, 1930–1960

1. Symons, Leslie. 'The agricultural industry, 1921–1962'. In Symons, Leslie. *Land Use in Northern Ireland* (London: University of London Press, 1963), p. 45.
2. Ibid., pp. 45, 47–48; Ministry of Agriculture of Northern Ireland (MANI), *Monthly Reports* (Belfast: HMSO, 1934–6).
3. MANI, op. cit., June 1935, pp. 6–7.
4. Symons, op. cit., p. 49.
5. MANI, op. cit., September 1943, pp. 188–9.
6. Ibid., July 1942, p. 117.
7. Ibid., December 1944, pp. 255–6.
8. Testimony of Mrs Mary Jane (Mamie) McQuoid and Mr James McKeown, UFTM tape R2004.4.
9. Harris, Rosemary. *Prejudice and Tolerance in Ulster* (Manchester: Manchester University Press, 1972), p. 18.
10. MANI, op. cit., September 1943, p. 230.
11. Ibid., July 1943, p. 73.
12. Ibid., p. 109; Symons, op. cit., p. 51.
13. MANI, op. cit., March 1945, p. 326.
14. Ibid., p. 230.
15. Northern Ireland Ploughing Association minutes, 7 April 1938.
16. Ibid., 18 May 1938.
17. Ibid., 28 July 1939.
18. Ibid., 29 December 1943.
19. Ibid., 2 February 1945.
20. MANI, op. cit., 1945.
21. Mogey, John M. *Rural Life in Northern Ireland* (London: Oxford University Press, 1947), pp. 40, 131.
22. MANI, op. cit., October 1944, p. 171.
23. Symons, op. cit., pp. 51–2.
24. Ibid., p. 54.

Chapter 3: Farm produce

1. Thomas, D.E.L. 'Farm types and farm incomes'. In Symons, op. cit., p. 162.
2. Ibid.
3. Ibid., pp. 162– 4.
4. Mogey, op. cit., p. 23.
5. Ibid., p. 96.
6. Ibid., p. 114.
7. Boal, F.W. 'County Down'. In Symons, op. cit., p. 230.
8. Ibid.
9. Bell, J. and Watson, M. *Irish Farming* (Edinburgh: Donald, 1986), pp. 57–8.
10. Sampson, G.V. *Statistical Survey of the County of Londonderry* (Dublin, 1802), p. 136.
11. Public Record Office of Northern Ireland (PRONI) D1513.
12. PRONI D1513/4/3.
13. Mogey, op. cit., p. 20.
14. Murphy, J.J. 'The mower from Moygannon'. *Ulster Folklife*, 12 (1996), p. 108.
15. Bell, J. 'A contribution to the study of cultivation ridges in Ireland'. *Journal of the Royal Society of Antiquaries of Ireland*, 114 (1984), pp. 80–97.

Chapter 4: Family farms

1. Thomas, D.E.L. 'Farm types and farm incomes'. In Symons, op. cit., pp. 171–2.
2. MANI, *Report on The Conditions of Employment of Agricultural Workers in Northern Ireland* (Belfast: HMSO, 1938), p. 8.
3. Harris, op. cit., p. 5.
4. Ibid, pp. 61, 64.
5. Ibid, pp. 53, 111.
6. Hannan, Damian. *Rural Exodus* (London: Chapman, 1970), p. 23.
7. Harris, op. cit., p. 32.

Chapter 5: The neighbours

1. Bell, J. 'Relations of mutual help between Ulster farmers'. *Ulster Folklife*, 24 (1978), pp. 48–58.
2. Harris, op. cit., pp. 70–71.
3. O'Dowd, Anne. *Meitheal* (Dublin: Comhairle Bhéaloideas Éireann, 1981).
4. Harris, op. cit., p. 106.
5. Thompson, Paul. The Voice of the Past: Oral History (Oxford: Oxford University Press, 1978), p. 131.
6. Mogey, op. cit., p. 116.
7. Ibid, p. 202.

Chapter 6: Hired help

1. Fitzpatrick, David. 'The disappearance of the agricultural labourer, 1841–1912'. *Economic and Social History*, 7 (1980).
2. *Report of the Proceedings of the Agricultural Wages (Regulation) Act (Northern Ireland) 1939 for the Two Years ended 31 December 1977* (Belfast: HMSO, 1978), p. 9.
3. MANI, op. cit., May 1942 , p. 43.
4. Ibid., November 1942, p. 268.
5. Ibid., March 1945, p. 326.
6. Ibid., December 1944, p. 226.
7. MANI, *Report on the Conditions of Employment of Agricultural Workers in Northern Ireland* (HMSO: Belfast, 1938).
8. Northern Ireland School Attendance Act, 1923; Saorstat Éireann School Attendance Act, 1926.
9. Nazareth Lodge Records.
10. PRONI Wage Book from Carse Hall for 1924.
11. On retirement, Mr and Mrs Drennan lived in a bungalow on the land of Miss Dorothy Robertson of the Dogleap. Mr Drennan kept up his interest in Clydesdale horses, acting as a judge at both local shows and shows in Britain. He died in 1981, having been predeceased by his wife Margaret, in 1979 (information from Mrs Margaret Collinson).
12. Micks, W.L. 'Baseline report for the Rosses'. In *History of the Congested Districts Board* (Dublin: Eason, 1925), p. 250. Baseline reports summarised living conditions in areas of Western Ireland taken over by the Congested Districts Board in the 1890s.
13. Langford Lodge was a well-known poultry farm in the 1930s. MANI, *Monthly Report*, September 1935, p. 33.
14. The figures in square brackets in the following paragraphs are corrections to John Magennis' figures, kindly provided by Mr Harry Jordan's son Henry.
15. Mogey, op. cit., p. 205.

Chapter 7: Recent history

1. Mogey, op. cit.
2. Ibid.
3. Harris, op. cit., p. 18.
4. Ibid., p. 128.
5. Symons, op. cit., pp. 48–9.
6. Ibid., p. 46.
7. Hannan, op. cit., p. 22.
8. Sweeney, Fionnuala. 'Women's work is never done'. *Causeway*, 1, no. (Belfast, 1994).
9. MANI, *Monthly Report*, October 1935, p. 43.
10. Berger, John. *Pig Earth* (London: Writers and Readers Publishing Co-operative, 1979).

Chapter 8: Oral testimony as history

1. Kavanagh, Gaynor. *Dream Spaces: Memory and the Museum* (London: Leicester University Press, 2000).
2. Ibid., p. 11.
3. Ibid., p. 15.
4. Ibid., p. 5.
5. Hobsbawm, Eric. *On History* (London: Weidenfeld & Nicholson, 1997), p. 206. Lowenthal, David. *The Past is a Foreign Country* (Cambridge: Cambridge University Press, 1985/1986), pp. 206–7.
6. Kavanagh, op. cit., p. 19.
7. Ibid., p. 56.
8. Ibid., p. 13.
9. Ibid., pp. 82–3.
10. Ibid., pp. 88–93.
11. Ibid., p. 45.
12. Hobsbawm, op. cit., pp. viii, 6.
13. Ibid., p. 17.
14. Kavanagh, op. cit., p. 4.
15. Sartre, J.-P. *Critique of Dialectical Reason* (trans. A. Sheridan-Smith) (London: New Left Books, 1976/1978), p. 34.
16. Ibid., p. 38.
17. Kavanagh, op. cit., p. 4.

Ferguson tractors ploughing in the 1930s (photograph courtesy of the Museum of English Rural Life)

Index

General